I know I put my glasses somewhere...

Lighthearted Devotions
with a Little Laughter...
because we might
as well embrace those
senior moments!

Inspired
by Faith

I know I put my glasses somewhere...
ISBN 978-0-9909508-2-0

Published by Product Concept Mfg., Inc.
2175 N. Academy Circle #200, Colorado Springs, CO 80909

Written and Compiled by Patricia Mitchell
in association with Product Concept Mfg., Inc.

All scripture quotations are from the King James version
of the Bible unless otherwise noted.

Scriptures taken from the Holy Bible,
New International Version®, NIV®.
Copyright © 1973, 1978, 1984 by Biblica, Inc.™
Used by permission of Zondervan.
All rights reserved worldwide.
www.zondervan.com

Sayings not having a credit listed are contributed by writers
for Product Concept Mfg., Inc. or in a rare case,
the author is unknown.

I know
I put my
glasses
somewhere...

You don't stop laughing when you grow old,
you grow old when you stop laughing.

George Bernard Shaw

It happens to all of us! Call them brain blips—those moments when we're stopped short by the realization that we drove home without recalling seeing a single landmark...when we notice that the silver streaks in our hair are not salon highlights...when the songs we grew up with have migrated to the oldies station.

Oh, yes...and there's more to come! But we're all in it together, so why not enjoy the ride? In these pages, you'll find bits of inspiration for perspective and nuggets of wisdom for pondering. There's friendly encouragement to look at the bright side of life, and lighthearted tales and whimsical quotes to keep you smiling all day long.

"Where did I leave my glasses?" It doesn't matter where you left them, or if you even own a pair. If you can see the humor of it all, you've got 20/20 vision!

It Just Clicked

Buy a new top-of-the line cell phone or computer, and six months later an upgrade comes out. Get comfortable with a different social media site, and then discover that the kids you want to communicate with are onto something else entirely. You get the idea—if it's new today, it's old tomorrow. Passé. Outdated.

For us, having the latest gadget might have mattered a decade or so ago, but there comes a time when status symbols lose their status. Now we're ready to take what's useful and leave the rest, and live happily ever after. We've reached that liberating stage of maturity where we're asking, "Do I really want a new cell phone?" instead of convincing ourselves that our friends will disown us if we don't get the latest one on the market.

Let's face it—now that grandparents have their own gadgets, they're no longer a badge of youth and cool-ness. When two-year-olds can outmaneuver us on the computer, it hardly matters whether we have version 1.0 or 10.0. We'll never catch up.

And that's okay. We can sit back and relax with the trusty old devices that are serving us well. The comfortable smile spreading across our face just might be the realization that for now at least, we've sidestepped yet another technological learning curve.

Remember when a web was a spider's home?

HENPECKED

A hen bought a new laptop, but was having trouble with a document. She called her neighbor over to take a look at it. "Easy," the second hen replied after examining the problem. "You've just got to double-cluck on it."

FROM THE MOUTHS OF BABES

Emma watched as her mother frantically searched her purse, pockets, car, and closet for her cell phone. As her mother enlarged the search area to the entire house, Emma said, "You know what they should invent, Mom? A cord that attaches the phone to a wall so you always know exactly where it is."

JUST WHAT YOU SAID

A computer user called tech support and told him what the problem was. "Okay," the agent said, "I need you to right-click."
"All right," replied the customer.
After a brief pause, the agent said, "Did you get a pop-up menu?"
"No."
"Then right-click again. Now do you see the pop-up menu?"
"No."
Baffled, the agent said, "Okay. Can you tell me exactly what you have done up to this point?"
"Sure," said the customer. "You told me to write Click and I wrote Click."

You might be spending a *little* more time online than you should if:

- *You've never actually met any of your friends face to face.*

- *At your last eye exam, the optician looked into your eyes and saw a screen saver.*

- *You choose restaurants based on whether they offer WiFi, not on the menu.*

- *You try to enter your password on the microwave.*

- *You can't communicate with anyone who's not online.*

- *You automatically add ".com" to the end of your sentences.*

- *You would rather give up chocolate than your computer.*

- *You can't pass a computer screen without stopping to check your email and social media page.*

- *You actually know what error pop-ups are telling you. And you successfully fix the problem.*

- *Tech support calls you for help!*

What's the Matter?

"Age is an issue of mind over matter," the humorist Mark Twain observed. "If you don't mind, it doesn't matter." His comment falls right along with the wisdom of not wasting your time trying to change what can't be changed. (Sure, you can lie about how old you are, but that won't budge the date of your birth certificate even by one day.)

But we can change our minds about what matters, and that's not the number of candles poking out of a heavily frosted layer cake. Now there are probably as many answers as to what matters as there are people pondering the question, but here's what those who have reached a grand old age most often mention: Love...faith...joy...gratitude...forgiveness...compassion... kindness. Not one of these great gifts lessens or is lost with the years. They'll never wear out, even with lifelong use. On the contrary, they grow, deepen, and are increasingly valued and appreciated as time goes on. We make things brighter for ourselves, and for those around us, when we know what matters.

Best of all, what matters is free, as available to teen-agers as to centenarians, and everyone in between. What matters has nothing to do with past or present circumstance. All it takes is a mind open to accept, embrace, and practice those things that only get better with age.

Middle age is when you choose your cereal for the fiber, not the toy.

*Don't be ashamed of your gray hair! Wear it proudly,
like a flag. You are fortunate, in a world of so many
vicissitudes, to have lived long enough to earn it.*
William Lyon Phelps

*I make the most of all that comes
and the least of all that goes.*
Sara Teasdale

*When people shake their heads because we are living
in a restless age, ask them how they would like to live
in a stationary one, and do without change.*
George Bernard Shaw

*Life is 10 percent what you make it,
and 90 percent how you take it.*
Irving Berlin

Grow old eagerly, triumphantly.
William Lyon Phelps

*Seek not that the things which happen should happen
as you wish; but wish the things which happen to be
as they are, and you will have a tranquil flow of life.*
Epictetus

THAT EXPLAINS IT

An irate customer called the newspaper office. "Where's my Sunday paper?" she demanded. "Ma'am, today is Saturday," the customer service agent said. "The Sunday paper won't be delivered until tomorrow, on Sunday."

After a rather lengthy pause, the customer replied in a sheepish tone of voice. "Well, I guess that explains why no one was in church this morning."

CASE DISMISSED

Two neighbors were involved in a long-running dispute, each woman accusing the other of causing trouble in their apartment building. They finally decided to take the issue to court for resolution. "Let's get to the evidence," the judge said to them. "I'll hear the oldest woman first."

The case was dismissed for lack of testimony.

NOT MY PROBLEM

Three friends were talking about the travails of getting on in age. One said, "Sometimes I open the refrigerator door and forget what it was I wanted to get." The second said, "I know how it feels. I've found myself standing on the landing of the stairs and not remembering whether I'm on my way up or down." "Thank goodness I don't have those problems—knock on wood," the third said as she rapped on the table. "Oh! That must be the door—I'll go see who it is."

No Energy? No Problem!

What's so good about being busy all the time? Nothing, that's what. Yet we're so intimidated by high-energy, multi-tasking, on-the-run folks that we figure we've got to keep up, or our reputation is dirt. But after a week of running around, we're tired. No, more than tired—utterly exhausted. Just a glance at tomorrow's to-do list of meetings, appointments, household tasks, along with a note to "fix gourmet dinner for eight tonight" brings us to the brink of tears.

Not to say the same thing doesn't happen to ultra-busy people, but they're not about to admit it. Instead they'll work all the harder and run all the faster. Head up another committee? Join a second exercise class? Tell the boss they'll be more than happy to work this weekend? Sure! Why not?

We know exactly why not, but we don't have to tell anyone that our get-up-and-go got up and went. Instead, we can loftily inform the hyper-active that we're taking a nap because we're in a dream-study program. No weeding the garden, because we're restoring natural habitat. We'd just as soon stay home tonight because we don't want to wear out the city streets. Anything will do.

Now take that nap and enjoy it!

When we borrowed customs from other countries, why didn't we borrow the siesta?

I like work; it fascinates me;
I can sit and look at it for hours.
Jerome K. Jerome

When ambition ends, happiness begins.
Proverb

Simplicity, simplicity, simplicity! I say, let your affairs
be as two or three, and not a hundred or a thousand.
Henry David Thoreau

Teach us delight in simple things.
Rudyard Kipling

It is not the man who has too little,
but the man who craves more, that is poor.
Seneca

ROLE REDUCTION

*A woman called a counselor asking if he would talk
to her husband. "What's the problem?" the counselor
asked.*

*"My husband thinks he's a big opera star. Every evening
he belts out the male lead in Carmen, Aida, Rigoletto,
La Traviata!"*

*"Send him around," the counselor said. "I'll see what I
can do."*

*The next week, the woman called the counselor again.
"I can't thank you enough," she said. "He's not singing
nearly as much anymore. How did you cure him of his
delusion?"*

*"I didn't," the counselor replied, "I simply gave him a
smaller role."*

WOOLLY REASON

*A state trooper saw a woman knitting and driving at the
same time. He rode up beside her and yelled, "Pull over!"*

"No, officer," she shouted, "it's mittens!"

TIME OFF

*One Sunday a minister decided to play hooky from
church. He called his assistant to fill in for him, and then
he set out for the lake and spent a glorious morning
fishing. St. Peter looked down from heaven and shook
his head. "You're not going to let him get by with this, are
you, God?"*

"Absolutely not," the Lord said.

*At that moment, the minister pulled up the catch of a
lifetime—a magnificent 10-pound bass.*

*"Hey," St. Peter exclaimed. "I thought you planned to
punish him!"*

*The Lord shrugged and with a smile, asked, "So who can
he brag to?"*

Bridge the Gaps

It will take you by surprise—the first time you have to honestly admit that you don't remember whether you took your daily prescription this morning...unplugged the coffee pot and hair curling wand before you left the house...changed the furnace filter lately.

At first, denial sets in. You never *used* to experience these memory-gaps, did you? Maybe you used to be on top of everything (or maybe not), but the fact is, things are different now. So now is the time to bridge the gap and then get on with your life. When it comes to issues, these are the smallest of the small and don't deserve one bead of sweat on your part.

Think about it. If you were the only one with a few memory-gaps, why are there several kinds of day-of-the-week pill boxes on your pharmacist's shelves? Buy one. Make believe it's for your mother, if it makes you feel better. Why do you think appliance timers were invented? Load up on several, and use them. And what's wrong with a note on the calendar for when it's time to replace filters, fertilize houseplants, and check your car's tire pressure? Nothing wrong at all.

You have better, more important, things to store in your head—like how revitalizing the sun feels on a clear, cloudless day...how fragrant the flowers are this spring... how beautiful the face is of your very best friend.

If you want to jog your memory,
take your laptop out for a run.

ONE OF THOSE MOMENTS

A maried couple realized that they were experiencing frequent memory lapses. To compensate, they decided to start writing things down. That evening, while watching TV, the wife asked her husband if he would get her a bowl of ice cream.

"Sure," he said as he got up from his chair.

"Don't you think you should write it down first?"

"No," he said, "something like a bowl of ice cream is simple enough to remember."

"Well, I'd also like you to add chocolate syrup and sprinkle nuts over it. You should be writing this down, honey."

But he insisted that he was fully capable of remembering ice cream, chocolate syrup, and nuts.

Twenty minutes later he returned with a plate of scrambled eggs, toast, and bacon and handed it to his wife.

"Dear," she sighed, "I told you to write it down. I said I wanted fried eggs."

OOOPS

Along a county lane, a trooper flags down a car that had been weaving all over the road. "Oh, thank goodness you're here," the frazzled driver says as she opens her window. "I almost had an accident! Suddenly I saw a tree right in front of me, and when I swerved to avoid it, there was another tree right in front of me!"

Reaching through the window to the rearview mirror, the officer says, "Ma'am, that's your air freshener."

It's Confidential—
Until Now

Confidence—that's what they said we needed. So we put on our game face, stood up straight, and strode into the job interview as if we were the most confident person in the world. We offered a firm handshake, made steady eye contract, spoke in an assertive tone of voice. Who were we fooling? Our stomach was in knots, with visions of breaking the interviewer into hysterics while feeding our résumé to the shredder.

Once on the job, we saw that everyone else appeared supremely confident, so we followed suit. Same with everything else that the years brought our way— parenting, committee work, group leadership. Confidence was crucial! Even if we had no idea what we were supposed to do.

Then came the time when we let down our guard. We all did. Maturity gave us the confidence to swap stories about not being able to sleep three days before our first day with the company...big meeting with the boss...presentation to a new client. We admitted to a few friends that child-raising had us bumbling along, hoping against hope that we were doing something right. And we realized right away that no one had any more confidence than we did.

We can drop the game face and confidently pat each other on the back, because we did pretty well after all.

Confidence is keeping your chin up;
overconfidence is sticking your neck out.

If we did all the things that we are capable of doing,
we would literally astound ourselves.
Thomas Edison

Go confidently in the direction of your dreams.
Live the life you have imagined.
Henry David Thoreau

God gives us always strength enough, and sense
enough, for everything He wants us to do.
John Ruskin

Be like the bird that, passing on her flight awhile on
boughs too slight, feels them give way beneath her,
and yet sings, knowing that she hath wings.
Victor Hugo

I am seeking. I am striving.
I am in it with all my heart.
Vincent van Gogh

I'M SURE!

Sue was delighted with her new hearing aid. "It works like a dream!" she enthused.
"Are you wearing it now?" asked her friend.
"Sure am. It's so comfortable, and I can hear perfectly!"
"What kind is it?"
"Two-thirty," Sue replied.

CONFIDENCE BUSTER

After sitting at the cosmetics counter and receiving a full make-up application from the sales associate, Linda left the department store feeling ten years younger. With her newly purchased products tucked into a bright shopping bag, she walked shoulders back, head held upright, happily smiling at other shoppers. That was until one approaching toddler piped up, "Hey, Mommy—look at the clown!"

MISPLACED CONFIDENCE

A man approaches God and says to Him, "You know, we really don't need You anymore. We've made huge scientific breakthroughs! Why we can even clone animals, and soon we'll be able to clone man, too."
"I see," replies God. "But I love you, and I want to make sure you can do without Me. Let's create life, okay?"
"You're on," says the man.
"So we'll do it the way I did in the old days, with Adam and Eve."
The man agrees; he reaches down to scoop up a handful of dirt.
"Whoa! Hold on there," God says. "You have to get your own dirt!"

Skill and confidence are an unconquered army.
George Herbert

*No passion so effectually robs the mind of all its
powers of acting and reasoning as fear.*
Edmund Burke

If one must, one can.
Proverb

*Risk! Risk anything! Care no more for the opinion of
others, for those voices. Do the hardest thing on earth
for you. Act for yourself. Face the truth.*
Katherine Mansfield

*As soon as you trust yourself,
you will know how to live.*
Johann von Goethe

*Believe that with your feelings and your work you
are taking part in the greatest; the more strongly you
cultivate this belief, the more will reality and the world
go forth from it.*
Rainer Maria Rilke

The Advice Not Taken

Have you ever actually followed someone else's advice? If you're like many people, the answer is a loud, resounding *No!* Even if you suspected deep down in your heart that the advice-giver was absolutely correct, you didn't take it. Instead, you did your own thing—and now wish you had taken the proffered advice.

Who wants to admit that someone else might be smarter, savvier, more mature, more experienced than ourselves? Advice from others makes us feel vulnerable, unmasked. Where we imagined we were following our dreams, doing what we had to do, our elders saw that we were headed straight to the edge of a cliff. Blindfolded. But take advantage of well-meant warnings? No way.

We've reached a point now where we're less apt to be advice-getters than advice-givers. We've gone through the school of hard knocks, and we feel well-qualified for the role. Under our collective belt, we have hard-earned know-how to draw on and our share of practical wisdom gleaned from personal experience, our friends' experience, and our friends' friends experience (including urban legends). We've been there and done that...often several times.

So why won't the young set listen when we try to tell them something? What makes them think they know more than someone twenty, thirty, forty years older than they? Why won't they simply take our advice?

Good advice is no better than poor advice,
unless you follow it.

USEFUL INFORMATION

"I hate talking cars," said Bob to his buddy. "Here this voice comes out of nowhere to tell you that your door's ajar."

"Yeah," replied his buddy. "Better if they told you something useful, like 'There's a speed trap up ahead.'"

SHE SAID WHAT?

A man's car stalled on a rural road. When he got out and lifted the lid, a cow ambled over and eyed the engine. "It looks like your engine overheated," the cow said. The man was so startled that he ran down the road until he met a farmer. He told the farmer what had happened.

"Was she a large red cow with a brown spot over one eye?" the farmer asked.

"That's right," the man replied.

"Oh, then don't listen to her," the farmer said. "She knows nothing about cars."

JUST WANT TO KNOW

A shy fellow went to the library and checked out a book called How to Hug. When he got home and sat down to read, he discovered he had volume seven of the encyclopedia.

Advice is like castor oil, easy enough to give but dreadful uneasy to take.
Josh Billings

Anybody can give advice—the trouble comes in finding someone interested in using it.

The best way to get your kids to take your advice is to find out what they plan to do, and then advise them to do it.

The true secret of giving advice is, after you have honestly given it, to be perfectly indifferent whether it is taken or not, and never persist in trying to set people right.
Hannah Whitall Smith

Advice is like snow; the softer it falls, the longer it dwells upon, and the deeper it sinks into the mind.
Samuel Taylor Coleridge

Many people want to serve God— but only in an advisory capacity.

Advice to ponder...

- Try not to drop your contact lens when you're in a crowded tap dancing class.

- Never promise a farm family that you'll water their plants and feed their animals while they're on vacation.

- Don't take up cross-country skiing unless you live in a very small country.

- When you start looking like your passport photo, you need a vacation.

- During an auction, refrain from waving to your friend across the room.

- Don't try to put on a fuzzy turtleneck sweater while eating a caramel apple.

- If you want to forget your troubles, walk around the block wearing tight shoes.

- In chemistry class, don't lick the spoon.

- To prevent hitting your thumb while hammering, have someone else hold the nails.

- The best gift for someone who has everything is a good burglar alarm.

- If you want to find something lost around the house, buy a replacement.

Born to Be Free

Transitions are scary. They throw us into situations we've never faced before—like the first day of school, first date, first job, first child. But without these transitions, we couldn't ever get an education, have a relationship, earn our own way in the world, or start a family. So we welcome them, though with some amount of anxiety, because they promise us very good things.

Then comes the completely uninvited transition. Employment disappears, and we're "out of a job." Kids go off to college or get their own place, and we have an "empty nest." Our working years draw to a close, and we're "in retirement." The phrases ring as appealingly as a dull thud, and for many, they bring life to a screeching halt. "What now?" we wail.

Freedom now, that's what. Rid of yesterday's role—in the home or in the workplace—you have the freedom to occupy a new one. What you've dreamed of doing, you can actually think about doing. Explore new paths, new ways to do things, new ways of living, of being. Whether the transition was planned or unplanned, fairly painless or the worst thing that's happened to you in recent memory, it's here now. It has happened, and you got through it.

So what now? Give yourself the freedom to fly!

The world changes so fast these days
that you couldn't stay wrong
all the time if you tried.

Progress is impossible without change;
and those who cannot change their minds
cannot change anything.
George Bernard Shaw

Today is not yesterday. We ourselves change; how
can our works and thoughts, if they are always to be
the fittest, continue always the same?
Thomas Carlyle

Did you hear about the little rural town where nothing
every changes? The local radio station is still running
last year's weather forecasts.

The only kind of change we really like
is the kind that jingles in our pocket.

Trouble creates a capacity to handle it.
Oliver Wendell Holmes, Jr.

WHY WE GET TAKE-OUT

Two college students were talking about the challenge of learning how to cook. "I've got a cookbook," one said, "but I've never been able to do anything with it."
"Was it too demanding?" asked the friend.
"Absolutely. Every single recipe begins the same way—Take a clean dish."

AT LAST

A group of distance runners were on the final mile of their race. The last runner was lagging more and more behind, prompting the second-to-last runner to look back mockingly. "Say, how's it feel to be the last guy?" he called with a laugh.
"I'll let you know," the last runner shouted. And promptly dropped out of the race.

IT'S HEAVENLY

A cat and a mouse died and went to heaven on the same day. One day God saw the mouse and asked how things were going so far. "Great," replied the mouse. "Only I wish I had a pair of in-line skates."
"No problem," God said, and He gave the mouse the skates.
The next day, God saw the cat and asked, "So, how do you like heaven so far?"
"Fantastic," the cat said, "and what a great surprise when last night's dinner rolled right up to me."

Out of Control

Our well-being depends on some level of control over ourselves and our personal space. Let's face it, when we give in to impulsive outbursts, we do nothing for our reputation, much less our relationships. When we're caught in events or situations completely beyond our ability to change, we feel bewildered and helpless.

So, yes, control is essential; but some of us want too much of it, and that's where trouble begins. Self-control is hard enough, and when we've mastered it, we have something worthwhile. But when we try to control someone else, we're in for a far tougher job—an impossible one, actually. In the attempt, we're stressed because strong-arming others is exhausting, 24/7 work. When we fail—and we will, sooner if not later—we'll fuss and fume and scream and yell... completely out of control.

Same for the world around us. Wise we are when we know the difference between those lives and events we can change and influence for the better, and those we need to leave alone. In many instances that affect us, God reserves to Himself the power to control the outcome.

Your control-duties begin with you. But do you know where they end?

I found peace of mind the minute I resigned as general manager of the universe.

28

"Knock, knock."
"Who's there?"
"Control freak. Now you say, 'Control freak who?'"

*Anyone who uses the phrase "as easy as taking
candy from a baby" has never tried to take candy
from a baby.*

*Believe there is a great power
silently working all things for good,
behave yourself and never mind the rest.*
Beatrix Potter

*It seems you can go anywhere you want
if you're dressed in a lab coat, look serious,
and carry a clipboard.*

*The secret of my success is that at an early age I
discovered I was not God.*
Oliver Wendell Holmes, Jr.

Not being able to govern events, I govern myself.
Michel de Montaigne

Self-command is the main elegance.
Ralph Waldo Emerson

Shopping Spree

Imagine walking into your favorite boutique and picking out the ugliest dress for yourself that you can find... or going into a department store and purposely buying a bottle of rancid cologne...or browsing Internet ads for an appliance that doesn't work. Highly unlikely, right? Right, unless you're in the market for a white elephant gift.

But when it comes to our thoughts, we easily grab whatever pops into our mind. Though they might be mean, unkind, or negative thoughts, we take them home anyway. Of course we know that these mind-fillers don't really work for us, because they make us feel down in the dumps, and then we start seeing everything in a negative light. All we start talking about is what's wrong with ourselves, everyone around us, and the whole world in general. Yet we pick these unhelpful "products" day after day, year after year.

Now is the time to throw away old, useless, and prickly thoughts and replace the junk with productive, meaningful, and decidedly upbeat "merchandise" for the mind. Pick out what's not only true, but helpful and attractive. Select, among everything out there, thoughts that will work to make your corner of the world brighter and cheerier. Go on a shopping spree with this one. And select only the best for yourself—you deserve it.

Cast your bread upon the water,
believing it will be returned to you
toasted and buttered.

LOOKING ON THE BRIGHT SIDE

"Someone complimented me on my driving today,"
Missy told her dad. "They left a note on my windshield
that says Parking Fine."

A nutritionist told me that I shouldn't eat ice cream for
dessert anymore...so now I have it for an appetizer.

"My boss told me I gave a dynamite performance!"
the young exec told his friends.
"At least I figure that's what she meant
when she said that I really bombed out there."

The optimistic fisherman is the one who takes along
a camera and a frying pan.

When she was in school, she read nothing except
mystery books—algebra, history, political science,
economics...

Optimism: a cheerful frame of mind that enables a tea
kettle to sing though in hot water up to its nose.

MAYBE IT WILL EVEN WORK FASTER!

The barista accidently spilled coffee on a customer's laptop keyboard. After emitting a few popping sounds, the screen went blank. The barista quickly wiped up the mess, apologized profusely, and added: "Omigosh, I sure hope it still works."

"It should," the customer replied as he restarted the device. "That was a double espresso."

TIMELY WARNING

The boss sees an employee show up late for work. Walking over to the guy's cubicle, the boss stood for several minutes watching the employee leisurely hang up his jacket and get out a few files from his desk. Just as he was about to go get a cup of coffee from the lunchroom, his boss yelled, "You should have been here an hour ago!"

"How come?" the employee asked, "what happened here an hour ago?"

PROBLEM?

Two friends, one an optimist and the other a pessimist, could never agree on any topic of conversation. Now the optimist owned a hunting dog that could walk on water. He decided to take the pessimist and the dog out duck hunting in a boat. When they got to the middle of the lake, the optimist spotted a duck. "Go, Rover," the man said. With that, the dog immediately jumped out of the boat, walked across the water, retrieved the duck, and walked back to the boat. "What do you say to that?" the optimist asked his friend.

The pessimist replied, "So your dog can't swim, can he?"

Dream lofty dreams, and as you dream,
so shall you become. Your vision is the promise
of what you shall at last unveil.
John Ruskin

Man's real life is happy, chiefly because
he is ever expecting that it soon will be so.
Edgar Allen Poe

The greater part of our happiness or misery depends
upon our dispositions, and not upon our circumstances.
Martha Washington

Could we change our attitude, we should not only see
life differently, but life itself would come to be different.
Life would undergo a change of appearance because
we ourselves had undergone a change in attitude.
Katherine Mansfield

Nothing can stop the man with the right mental
attitude from achieving his goal; nothing on earth can
help the man with the wrong mental attitude.
Thomas Jefferson

Fill 'Er Up!

Enthusiasm is something we associate with the younger set. As years pass, it can feel as if our earlier enthusiasm for music, dance, reading, sports, and just plain living has drained away. We didn't even realize it was gone until one day we heard a child oooh and ahhh at the sight of a rainbow...a teenager chatter excitedly about her favorite team, her latest accomplishments, her hopes for the future. What happened to our ability to wonder? What happened to our enthusiasm for doing things and grabbing hold of new experiences?

If your level of enthusiasm is running low, here are a few reasons you might want to fill 'er up. First, enthusiasm enhances life. It makes the world more colorful, more interesting. Without enthusiasm, you're only going through the motions, no matter what you're doing or why. Second, enthusiasm fortifies and strengthens the one who embraces it. It makes you better able to get through bad times, because enthusiasm keeps you buoyant and purposeful. It allows you to more fully enjoy good times, because it engages you with life. Third, enthusiasm is contagious. An enthusiastic person is not only interested, but interesting. There's no better way to become enthusiastic than to hang around enthusiastic people.

Enthusiasm isn't just for kids. It's for you. So fill 'er up!

It's good to take pleasure in the simple things in life... like seeing the driver who sped past you at 80 miles an hour get pulled over by the highway patrol two miles down the road.

GO FOR IT!

"What starting salary are you expecting?" the interviewer asked the newly minted college grad. Going for it, the grad said, "Something in the $150,000 range, depending on the benefits package."
"All right," said the interviewer. "So how about six weeks' vacation, 14 paid holidays, full medical and dental insurance, 100% company match for your 401(k), plus a company car for your personal use?"
The grad's eyes lit up with excitement. "Wow, are you kidding?"
"Sure am," the interviewer replied, "But you started it."

WHO'S CALLING?

With his wife suddenly in labor, a man frantically called 911. "My wife is having a baby!" he shouted to the dispatcher. "What am I supposed to do?"
The dispatcher told him to calm down, and then she asked, "Is this her first child?"
"No!" he yelled, exasperated. "This is her husband!"

None are so old as those
who have outlived enthusiasm.
Henry David Thoreau

Enthusiasm is the greatest asset in the world.
It beats money and power and influence.
Henry Chester

Nothing great was ever achieved without enthusiasm.
Ralph Waldo Emerson

No one keeps up his enthusiasm automatically.
Enthusiasm must be nourished with new actions,
new aspirations, new efforts, new vision.

Exuberance is beauty.
William Blake

Get Comfortable

"Comfortable in her own skin" is the first impression people get when they meet her. Or him. And that's wonderful for her or him, because most of us are decidedly *uncomfortable* in, with, or about our skin. We deem it wrinkly, or splotchy, or blemished, or the wrong shade, or that there's too much of it. We go to great expense to change it, shape it, tan it, or cover it up. Think of the time, money, and stress we'd save if we simply got comfortable in our own skin!

Actually, skin-comfort begins where skin isn't—and that's in the heart and mind. If we constantly judge ourselves, we'll always find something wrong with who we are on the outside and on the inside. If we're forever downplaying what we do or finding no real value in the God-created person we are, we'll never feel happy with ourselves.

Do you want to change all that? Then get comfortable. Get comfortable knowing that you're trying your best, but you're not perfect (and neither is anyone else)...that you are who you are...that God doesn't make mistakes...that He loves you dearly, so there's no good reason for you not to love yourself. And your skin is just fine. Settle into it as you would wiggle into a soft, warm easy chair. Let you be the one who's comfortable in your own skin.

As Noah's wife once told him, "I'd feel a lot more comfortable if those two termites were in a glass container."

He who undervalues himself is
justly undervalued by others.
William Hazlitt

How can we send the highest love to another
if we do not have it for ourselves?
Prentice Mulford

He who seeks for applause only from without
has all his happiness in another's keeping.
Oliver Goldsmith

Do not wish to be anything but what you are.
Francis de Sales

DAY'S WORK

At creation, God was talking to one of his angels. He said:
"I've just made a 24-hour period of alternating light and darkness on Earth."
"That's wonderful," the angel exclaimed. "So what are you going to do now?"
And God replied: "I think I'll call it a day."

DOWN ON THE FARM

Two farmers, Tom and Bob, met at an agricultural convention. After talking about his small rural spread in a neighboring state, Tom said, "So tell me about your farm."
Swelling with pride, Bob launched into a description. "Let me put it this way: I can get in my truck at dawn, spend the day on my land, and still not cover it all by nightfall!"
"I understand," drawled Tom. "You know, I used to have a truck like that."

QUITE RESPONSIBLE

"In this job," the interviewer said, "we need someone who's responsible."
"That's me," the applicant announced. "In my last job, whenever anything went wrong, they said I was responsible."

DOG DAYS

Neighborhood dog owners started arguing about whose dog was the smartest. After several doggy feats were mentioned, one owner spoke up and said, "Every morning, my dog waits at the edge of the driveway for the paper carrier. When the guy pulls up and throws the paper, my dog gives him a tip, grabs the paper, and brings it into me."
"I know all about that!" shouted another owner.
"How do you know?"
"Because my dog told me."

What's So Funny?

Don't you just love it when someone tries to jolly you out of a bad mood? Take the clerk at the grocery store who thinks he's a stand-up comic. But you don't *feel* like hearing jokes, much less laughing at them. You're in a hurry, you didn't get your cup of coffee before leaving the house, and you're wondering if there's enough in your bank account to pay for the groceries that Mr. Laugh-a-Minute is so merrily ringing up.

And how about the friend who always has a bright, chirpy response to your latest personal gripe? She thinks she's making you feel better. You're supposed to smile and admit that what you were complaining about really is no big deal at all—but to you, *it's a big deal!* Otherwise you would have laughed in the first place.

Of course, the hardest thing for any of us to admit is that these people—the jolly clerk, the cheerful friend—are right. They have their bad days, too, but they've figured out that humor lifts the spirit, sparks upbeat thinking, delivers a better outlook, and gets the mind off one's self for a few minutes. And not just for the humor-receiver, but the humor-giver, too.

Go ahead, roll your eyes at the corny jokes. Nod patiently at the well-intentioned platitudes. And then do both of you a favor—laugh out loud.

If you would like to spoil the day for a grouch, give him a smile.

There is no duty we so much underrate
as the duty of being happy.
Robert Louis Stevenson

Humor is the great thing, the saving thing, after all.
The minute it crops up, all our hardnesses yield,
all our irritations and resentments flit away,
and a sunny spirit takes their place.
Mark Twain

Cheerfulness keeps up a kind of daylight in the mind,
and fills it with a steady and perpetual serenity.
Joseph Addison

A person without a sense of humor is like a wagon
without springs—jolted by every pebble in the road.
Henry Ward Beecher

GUARANTEED GROANERS

What happened to the survivors of a collision between a red ship and a blue ship? – They were marooned.

Did you hear about the man who fell into an upholstery machine? –He's fully recovered now.

Why does eating fish increase brain-power? – Because it travels in schools.

What do you get when you divide the circumference of a pumpkin by its diameter? – Pumpkin pi.

Did you hear about the cat that swallowed a skein of yarn? – She had mittens.

What's guaranteed to take care of baldness? – Hair.

What business can't thrive without strikes? – Baseball.

Why did the scientist disconnect his doorbell? – Because he wanted to win the Nobel Prize.

Did you hear about the dog that gave birth to her puppies by the side of the road? – She was ticketed for littering.

How do skeletons study for their exams? – They bone up on the facts.

Did you hear about the skunk that went to church? – He had his own pew.

When is an eye not an eye? – When an onion makes it water.

FULL LOAD

A man appears at the Pearly Gates dragging a heavy trunk behind him. "Hold on there," St. Peter says. "You can't bring that in."

"I've got to," the man replies.

"What could you possibly have in there that's better than what awaits you in heaven?" St. Peter asks.

The man opens the trunk to reveal 100 neatly stacked gold bricks.

St. Peter looks and then breaks out in laughter. "So," he exclaims, "you brought pavement?"

SWEET MIRACLE

One evening a woman discovered her husband standing over their newborn's cradle. She saw him looking down at the sleeping infant with an expression on his face of happiness, awe, amazement, and delight. Because he rarely showed emotion, she was touched. Slipping her arms around his waist, she whispered, "A penny for your thoughts."

"It's unbelievable," he said with a big smile. "I can't believe a cradle of this good quality cost us only $24.99!"

SHORT ANSWER

It was mealtime on a trans-Atlantic flight. The flight attendant slowly made her way down the aisle with her tray-laden trolley. "Would you like dinner, sir?" she asked one of the passengers.

"What are my choices?" the passenger asked.

"Yes or no," she replied.

Best Guest

Who would happily throw open the door of her home to a sour, dour, and thoroughly negative person? Many of us do exactly that when we fall into ingratitude. As bad company goes, this one takes the prize.

Gratitude, however, is a much more desirable guest. Welcome Gratitude, and Ingratitude slithers out the back way, and good riddance. When Gratitude gets comfortable in your home and heart, instantly your problems seem lighter and easier to handle. That's because Gratitude starts naming everything you have that you love. What are these things, anyway? One by one, start thinking about them and notice how your sack gets fuller and fuller, and even spills over. Problems? Well, they could fit in a tea bag when you start comparing containers.

Just being in the presence of Gratitude clarifies your thoughts, and you find you actually come up with solutions to problems. Gratitude stirs you to drop irritation and annoyance as your go-to response to life's minor frustrations. And when you stop letting small things bug you, you feel better. "Things aren't so bad," you admit to Gratitude, who looks for all the world like she'll stay for the long haul. And voilà! Life is good.

The wise count their blessings; fools, their problems.

When you arise in the morning,
think of what a precious privilege it is to be alive—
to breathe, to think, to enjoy, to love.
Marcus Aurelius

Reflect upon your present blessings,
of which every man has many;
not on your past misfortunes, of which all men have some.
Charles Dickens

The person who has stopped being thankful
has fallen asleep in life.
Robert Louis Stevenson

No duty is more urgent than that of returning thanks.
James Allen

Some people complain because God put
thorns among roses, while others praise Him
for putting roses among thorns.
Author Unknown

WHAT YOU DON'T KNOW...

The father of two daughters was prepared to find something to criticize about every young man who came to the door to take them out. But each time his daughters introduced him to their dates, he was pleasantly surprised and immensely grateful. The young men were polite, well-groomed, and well-spoken. Years later, the father mentioned this to his daughters and praised their maturity and good taste. The eldest exchanged a knowing look with her sister, and then said: "Well, Dad, we didn't exactly bring around everyone we went out with."

MOMENTARY BONUS

A teacher was trying to teach addition to her young student. "Look, Tom," she said. "Imagine you reached into your pocket and took out a nickel. Then you reached into your other pocket and took out another nickel. How much would you have?"
The boy brightened, then grew somber. "Someone else's pants," he said.

THANKS FOR THE WARNING

Entering a mom-and-pop store, a new customer saw a sign saying, "Beware of the dog." He looked around, but all he could see was an old, harmless-looking dog fast asleep by the side of the door. The customer said to the clerk at the counter, "Is he the dog I need to be afraid of?"
"Sure is," said the clerk.
"He sure doesn't look very dangerous to me. Why did you put that sign up?"
"Because everyone keeps tripping over him."

Be thankful for...

- The start of every day. You have made it this far, and now you have a chance to go even further.

- Your present challenges, because it is through them that you gain knowledge, strength, and plain old know-how.

- Your present blessings, because they are gifts granted to you by a loving and compassionate God, and they are meant to sweeten the way.

- People and places you see every day...family and friends...familiar landmarks...kind strangers...helpful neighbors...the place you call home.

- Things around you that you usually take for granted...fresh water...favorite foods...dependable utilities...paved roads...treasured possessions...a roof over your head.

- Feelings of tenderness, compassion, and love... the ability to dream, to remember, to share... the awesome reality of being alive at this time, this moment.

- The end of every day. You have done all you were able to do, and now it is time to give thanks, forgive, and let go. Go to sleep with a heart and mind at peace.

Blurred Vision

For those among us who have worn glasses since the first day of school, it's no big deal. But for others, whose 20/20 vision has stuck with them through the years, it comes as an unpleasant surprise: our sight isn't as sharp as it used to be. Things have started looking a little blurry. First we buy glasses for reading menus...then glasses for driving...and then glasses for seeing the wall right in front of us.

Unlike in our grade-school days, however, glasses are now fashionable. They're In. You can find glasses bedecked with color, bling, and sparkle. Or you can forget about glasses and wear contacts. Any way you do it, your sight is back to sharp, and you're happy.

But here's a case for welcoming blurred vision— the kind that comes to us after we've gained some experience in this life, and it's the best kind there is. With maturity, our inner eyes are less keen than before to scrutinize the faults of others...less likely to view the world in black and white...less apt to examine every question from one vantage point—our own.

While certain things become blessedly blurred, here's what gets sharper and sharper: our ability and willingness to perceive what's strong and lasting in life, like hope and humor, grace and forgiveness, love and laughter. At last, our eyes begin to see what really counts.

Nowadays the woman with her ear to the ground is simply looking for her contact lens.

SEE?

A student asked her college professor why he had three pairs of glasses. He explained: "I have one pair for reading, one pair for distance vision, and the third pair for looking for the other two."

EYE TEST

Optometrist: Have your eyes been checked?
Patient: No, they've always been blue.

SHARP SIGHT

Her daughter walked up to her mom and started staring at her hair. After a few minutes, the child said, "Mommy, how come some parts of your hair are gray?"
Mom thought she could turn this into a teachable moment, so she replied: "Every time you misbehave, I get a gray hair."
The little girl pondered the matter. Then she said, "Mom?"
"Yes?"
"How come Grandma's hair is all gray?"

INSIGHT

At a gala event, an elegant older lady challenged a young man to guess her age. "You must have some idea of how old I am," she said.
"I have several ideas," the man said with a smile, "but I don't know whether to make it ten years younger because of your looks or ten years older because of your intelligence."

What we see depends mainly on what we look for.
John Lubbock

The world is a looking glass and gives back
to every man the reflection of his own face.
Frown at it and it will in turn look sourly upon you;
laugh at it and with it, and it is a jolly, kind companion.
William Makepeace Thackeray

The eye sees what it brings the power to see.
Thomas Carlyle

Dwell on the beauty of life.
Watch the stars, and see yourself running with them.
Marcus Aurelius

People only see what they are prepared to see.
Ralph Waldo Emerson

To see a world in a grain of sand,
And a heaven in a wild flower,
Hold infinity in the palm of your hand,
And eternity in an hour.
William Blake

How to See Better at Any Age

1. We're quick to see what's wrong with the world.
   While there are many problems among us, dwelling
   on them won't help. Consciously and mindfully
   focus your eyes on what is pleasant, pleasing, and
   beautiful; it will lift your spirits and fill your heart
   with hope. Only then will you have the insight it
   takes to see what you can make better.

2. Discover new things without going anyplace new.
   Look at your home, your surroundings, and all
   creation as if for the first time. Focus on familiar
   faces and really listen to what people are saying as
   if you have never heard their voice before.

3. Realize that you never know everything that's
   behind the behavior, reactions, and responses of
   others. Only God sees inside the heart, examines
   the mind, and knows all that has happened in
   someone's life.

4. Look with compassion on all.

5. Focus on your abundance instead of your lack.

6. Never compare yourself to others and allow envy to
   cloud your vision. See the best in yourself and see
   the best in others.

7. Accept reality, and watch how it opens opportunity,
   often through misfortune...creates change, even
   when we think our situation will never change...
   never fails to surprise and delight, if only we would
   open our eyes to see it.

Sole Worry

You've heard about the fellow who, lying in bed, hears his upstairs neighbor drop one shoe with a loud thud. Our fellow then spends a sleepless night waiting for the other shoe to drop! It never does—maybe his noisy neighbor decided to quiet down...or was so tired that he fell into bed with one shoe on...or...well, there are all sorts of reasons why the wakeful man never heard the other shoe drop.

When we toss and turn all night with our minds in a whirr worrying about what could, might, or probably will happen, we're like the restless fellow, anticipating in nerve-shattering fear of what's next. We figure that one problem must mean a second is right on its heels...a single serious issue certainly brings several even more-serious ones in its wake.

Name something that has worried you in the past. Did it take place? Probably not. And even if it did, ask yourself how much your worry contributed toward confronting, coping with, or resolving the situation. The answer is "nothing."

Worry is habit forming. One or two nights spent waiting for the other shoe to drop turns into three or four. Before you know it, worry is your ever-present bedtime companion.

Let the shoe drop when and where it may. Enjoy the day and sleep well tonight.

***Worry is interest paid
on trouble before it falls due.***

Funny you should worry...

- Today is the tomorrow you worried about yesterday.

- If you worry about what might be, and wonder what might have been, you ignore what is.

- Worry throws "faith in God" out the window.

- People who worry are spending time gathering sticks to build bridges they will never need to cross.

- Worry gives a small thing a big shadow.

- To expect life to be tailored to your specifications is to invite trouble.

- Worry doesn't help tomorrow's troubles, but it does take away today's happiness.

- A problem not worth praying about is not worth worrying about.

- Worry is a complete cycle of inefficient thought revolving around a pivotal fear.

What madness is it to be expecting evil
before it comes.
Seneca

It only seems as if you are doing something
when you worry.
Lucy Maud Montgomery

There are people who are always anticipating trouble,
and in this way they manage to enjoy many sorrows
that never really happen to them.
Josh Billings

If you see ten troubles coming down the road,
you can be sure that nine will run into the ditch
before they reach you.
Calvin Coolidge

The sovereign cure for worry is prayer.
William James

I am an old man and have had many troubles, most of which never happened.
Author Unknown

Some of your hurts you have cured,
And the sharpest you still have survived—
But what torments of grief you endured
From the evil which never arrived.
Ralph Waldo Emerson

Worry never climbed a hill,
worry never paid a bill,
Worry never dried a tear,
worry never calmed a fear.
Worry never darned a heel,
worry never cooked a meal,
It never led a horse to water,
nor ever did a thing it oughter.
Author Unknown

Worry is a futile thing—
It's somewhat like a rocking chair.
Although it keeps you occupied,
It doesn't get you anywhere.
Author Unknown

Living Standard

At a certain point, it's easy to leave a few, if not all, of those youthful ideals behind. With years of real-life experience behind us, we admit that we've often fallen short of our highest hopes for ourselves. Somehow our parents' failings seem more than forgivable; if we haven't done the same things ourselves, we can understand what they did and why. We're never as good as we'd like to be; and we discover along the way that others aren't as good as we'd like them to be, either.

Yet without holding onto high ideals and striving to live up to them, our character suffers. We start not caring about something that we need to care about. Yes, we know we'll never reach perfection in this world, and neither will anyone else. But the intention and act of reaching for the best in ourselves keeps us alive, vibrant, and engaged with growth and productive effort. Expecting the best from others frees us to communicate with the people we meet not with suspicion and skepticism, but with kindness and generosity. Certainly, unless we set high ideals for ourselves, we have no business expecting them from others...and we won't get them, either.

Real-life experience and ideals can walk hand in hand...and we can walk right along with them.

> *Nothing is more contagious*
> *than a bad example.*

People never improve unless they look to some
standard or example higher or better than themselves.
Tyron Edwards

There is transcendent power in example. We reform
others subconsciously, when we walk uprightly.
Anne Sophie Swetchine

It is reasonable to have perfection in our eye
that we may always advance toward it,
though we know it can never be reached.
Samuel Johnson

The first great gift we can bestow on others
is a good example.
Thomas Morell

People seldom improve when they have no model
but themselves to copy after.
Oliver Goldsmith

FAIR PLAY

*"It's been a long time since you and Bob have
played golf together," Tom's wife said. "Has something happened?"*
*"Sure has," Tom said. "I ask you, would you play
with someone who moves his ball closer to the
hole when he thinks no one's looking, deliberately
creates a distraction halfway through his teammate's
backswing, and lies about his handicap?"*
"Certainly not!" cried his wife.
"Well," Tom said, "neither will Bob."

TAXING TIME

*The owner of a pizza parlor was being questioned by
the IRS about his tax return. He had reported a net
profit of $80,000 for the year. The owner vehemently
defended himself, shouting, "I work from dawn to
dusk to make a living! Everyone in my family helps
out, and we close only two days a year. We have a
smart, efficient operation! And you want to know how
I made $80,000?"*
*"It's not the net income we're asking about," the
agent said. "It's these deductions for six trips for you,
your wife, and kids to go to the Bahamas."*
*"Oh that," the owner said, calming down. "I should
have explained—we deliver."*

Have Faith

Most of us bear a few scars from having put our faith in the wrong place. The person we depended on proved not so dependable after all...wealth we thought would see us through any calamity, didn't...the job, status, or position we imagined would bring happiness proved unable to deliver...ideas that sounded so solid way back then have grown worn, thin, and unable to meet today's needs.

Faith that stands the test of time is a gift. If you have it, give thanks! If you don't, it's not too late to receive it. Begin by having faith that your heavenly Father knows you by name and loves you dearly. No matter who you are or where you are, just knowing you are loved is essential to your sense of purpose...your joy...your serenity. And God's love is there for you.

Have faith that doing the right thing is the best thing, even when no one's looking. You will feel better about yourself. You will have earned the right to stand tall, walk with your head up, and look anyone in the eye. Have faith that if you treat others fairly and kindly, they are more than likely to treat you the same way. Have faith that things will work out, even if at the present moment, you can't imagine how.

Most importantly, have faith.

If overcome by doubt,
stop for a faith lift.

PICTURE THIS!

A news photographer was assigned to get some video of a gigantic forest fire. Because of the dense smoke at ground level, his editor hired a light plane for aerial views. The photographer was told that the plane would be waiting for him at a small rural airfield. So the photographer drove to the airfield and spied a small plane warming up on the runway. He parked the car, ran to the plane, jumped in and yelled, "Let's go!" Once in the air, the photographer shouted: "I want you to fly over the middle of the fire and get as low as you can get!"

"Why?" asked the pilot.

"What do you mean, why?" the exasperated photographer said. "I want to get some video of the fire for the news station!" With that, he flashed his employee ID card.

The pilot, now looking worried, quietly asked, "So you're not the instructor?"

CROSSED PATHS

A deer was trying to cross a busy road. After he had been standing for quite some time, a bear walked by and said, "Did you know that there's a zebra crossing down the street?"

"Well," replied the deer, "I sure hope he's having more success than I am!"

WHO IS GOD?

A preacher, in the middle of his impassioned sermon, bellowed, "Tell me, who is God?"
From the back pew, a little boy shouted, "God is a chauffeur!"
The preacher was stunned. "What made you say that, young man?" he asked.
Replied the boy: "Because He drove Adam and Eve out of the Garden of Eden."

KEEP THE FAITH

In the young couples' Bible class, the pastor talked about the story of Abraham and Sarah. Although well into old age before their son was born, they had faith in God's promise that they would have a child. The pastor asked the class, "What lesson can we take away from this story?"
A young mother of three who was having financial difficulties blurted out, "They were smart and waited until they could afford a baby!"

A MATTER OF TIME

A young man was lying on the grass and gazing up at the sky. Musing on the mysteries of life, he lifted his thoughts heavenward and asked, "How long is a million years?"
"Up here," St. Peter answered, "a million years is the same as a minute."
Impressed, the man posed a more earth-bound question: "Then how much is a million dollars?"
"Up here," St. Peter answered, "a million dollars is the same as a penny."
The man brightened. "Then you'll give me a penny?"
"Sure, in a minute."

Wealth of Experience

Some people have the Midas touch. They're the ones who hold a garage sale and sell old furniture for more than they paid for it in the first place. They manage to get a raise when everyone else's salary remains stagnant. Their investments shoot up in value quarter after quarter. They enter contests and win.

For most of us, it's "gain some, lose some." We might see impressive financial returns in one area, but find we've taken a loss in another. There's a place, however, where we can always turn a profit—and that's from our experiences. We benefit from positive experiences when we build on the knowledge of what brings us satisfaction, and when we draw on our awareness of what changes things for the better. When what we think, say, and do works for our good and the good of those we love, we want to repeat those things. Soon we have a wealth of positive experiences and golden memories.

Not-so-positive experiences are a valuable addition to our portfolio, too. When we're willing to learn, grow, and adapt from what happens to us, our know-how increases, wisdom builds, and character strengthens. We earn self-confidence and reap the reward of being able to help and comfort others, because we understand. We've been there.

Today, count your many experiences and smile—you are rich, indeed!

Money is like manure—of very little use unless it's spread around.

Money matters...

- I have enough money to last me for the rest of my life if I don't have to buy anything.

- Money talks. But all mine ever says is "good-bye."

- There's a foolproof way to save money—spend some one else's.

- He seems to be living in the past. And why not? It's a lot cheaper!

- Penny-pinchers aren't fun to live with, but they make great ancestors.

- It's no problem to meet expenses—everywhere I go, there they are.

- The buck stopped before it got here.

- Money doesn't grow on trees—you have to beat the bushes for it.

- The only way I can say I have folding money in my wallet is if they start making nickels with hinges.

- Those who are quick on the draw have little left in the checking account.

- A dollar may not go as far as it used to, but what it lacks in distance, it makes up in speed.

Money is in some respects like fire—
it is a very excellent servant but a terrible master.
P. T. Barnum

It's good to have money and the things that money
can buy, but it's good, too, to check up once in a
while and make sure that you haven't lost the things
that money can't buy.
George Horace Lorimer

October: This is one of the peculiarly dangerous
months to speculate in stocks. The others are July,
January, September, April, November, May, March,
June, December, August and February.
Mark Twain

The golden age only comes to men
when they have forgotten gold.
G. K. Chesterton

HOPE LEFT

Husband and wife were enjoying a South Sea cruise until the luxury liner was shipwrecked. The sole survivors, they were washed ashore on a deserted island. Day after day, they scanned the horizon, hoping to spot a passing vessel but none came. Time began to drag, and they started to think about their home back in the States, wondering if they'd ever see it again.

The wife asked, "Honey, did you remember to pay the loan on the SUV before we left?"

"No," her husband replied, "I forgot completely about it."

"Did you put the checks for the utility bills in the mail?"

"Sheesh, I forgot them, too," he said. "They're still sitting on the kitchen counter."

"How about the house payment?"

"No, dear. Sorry."

"And the quarterly tax bill?" the wife asked.

Husband shook his head. "I'm really sorry, dear."

His wife said after a pause: "Well, there's one good thing."

"What's that?"

"They're sure to find us."

GLAD TO HELP

A woman knocked on the door of a house. "I'm collecting for the city swimming pool," she told the homeowner. So the homeowner handed her two buckets of water.

Make Room!

If you have ever downsized your home, you've had to make some choices. You can't keep everything! Smaller—or fewer—rooms won't accommodate all the furniture and you might not have as many closets and cabinets for storage. In all likelihood, you'll go through your possessions carefully, keeping only those things that you treasure most and those that fit your new surroundings.

As we move into different stages of life, our "accommodations" change, too. If we go from one to another without deciding what we want to take with us, we'll simply drag along stuff we don't need anymore—for example, old habits that no longer reflect who we are...negative self-talk that ignores our talents, abilities, and accomplishments...long-held opinions that don't stand up to personal experience and mature scrutiny.

When you get rid of what you don't like and don't need, you open space for things you truly want to keep, like your strength of character, your ability to love, your happy memories. You make room for worth-while things like insight, grace, acceptance, peace, contentment, wisdom, and joy so they can grow and flourish.

Why burden yourself with what you're no longer using? Why not eliminate what you no longer need or treasure? Make room in yourself for the best you possess at this exciting stage of life.

If you correct yourself,
others won't need to.

*Many men go fishing all of their lives without knowing
that it is not fish they are after.*
Henry David Thoreau

The life which is unexamined is not worth living.
Socrates

*Wherever we are, it is but a stage
on the way to somewhere else; and whatever we do,
however well we do it, it is only a preparation
to do something else that shall be different.*
Robert Louis Stevenson

*Almost every man wastes part of his life
in attempts to display qualities which he does not
possess, and to gain applause which he cannot keep.*
Samuel Johnson

*The greatest thing in the world
is to know how to belong to oneself.*
Michel de Montaigne

It's About Time

During our growing-up years, it seemed as if time stretched out forever. A summer afternoon could lengthen into endless hours of play and rest, giggles and musings...the gap between the first day of school and the last day of school felt like a lifetime of study, books, classrooms, and essays. We counted the days before Christmas, each one seemingly longer than the last. The years until we were old enough to join the team, get a driver's license, graduate, find a place of our own couldn't get here fast enough.

How time has changed! Or at least our perception of it. We have discovered that we cannot take even a day, an hour, for granted—no one can. So some of us slow down and start smelling the roses...savoring relationships...asking ourselves what's meaningful rather than what others say we should do or what we have always done. Many among us create a bucket list of things we want to experience and places we want to see while we're still able to do so. We promise ourselves that we won't put off doing what's important to us, what personally means the most, because we know that God gives time as a gift, not a guarantee.

Fill this moment with the fullness of your presence. Inhabit time...use it...glory in the gift, the awesome miracle, of time.

Why is the third hand on a watch
called the second hand?

Many of our troubles come from too much time on our hands and not enough time on our knees.

Nothing arrives more slowly and passes more quickly than a vacation.

Half our life is spent trying to find something to do with the time we have rushed through life trying to save.
Will Rogers

If you think time heals everything, try waiting in a doctor's office.

By the time you get your shoulder to the wheel, your nose to the grindstone, and your ear to the ground, it's usually time for lunch.

Insurance agent: "Don't you want your office furnishings insured against theft?"
Business owner: "Yes, everything except the clock. Everyone watches that."

Time is like money: The less we have of it to spare, the further we make it go.
Josh Billings

Let me tell thee, time is a very precious gift of God;
so precious that He only gives it
to us moment by moment.
Amelia Barr

Know the true value of time! Snatch, seize, and enjoy
every moment of it. No idleness, no laziness,
no procrastination. Never put off until tomorrow
what you can do today.
Philip Chesterfield

We always have time enough
if we will but use it aright.
Johann von Goethe

Write it on your heart
that every day is the best day in the year.
Ralph Waldo Emerson

I always say to myself, what is the most
important thing we can think about at this
extraordinary moment?
François de La Rochefoucault

Take Time

Take time to work—
it is the price of success.
Take time to think—
it is the source of power.
Take time to play—
it is the secret of youth.
Take time to read—
it is the foundation of knowledge.
Take time to laugh—
it is the music of the soul.
Take time to be kind—
it is the hand of God.
Take time to pray—
it is the privilege of faith.
Author Unknown

Follow the Sun

Watch how blossoms lean toward the sunshine. Petals unfold to embrace the warmth and brightness of the sun's rays, whether sunbeams pour from the sky or sparkle through a windowpane. From whatever direction the sun beckons them, the flowers follow.

Sometimes we're not as smart as the sun-facing flowers. We let go of the activity or pastime that once made our imagination bloom. We turn away from where we discovered beauty, the hobby that brought so much color to our lives, to chase things we were told we must pursue. Often necessity, duty, or tradition pulls our focus in one direction, but our heart longs for its earlier and natural source of warmth and brightness.

Where did your heart used to find its sunshine? Maybe spending a lazy afternoon reading a book, but you rarely have that kind of time anymore. Why not make a little time—say 15 or 20 minutes a day to bask in the warmth of a book that sparks your imagination? Maybe you used to draw or paint, sew or scrapbook, listen to music or photograph landscapes, but you don't do it anymore. If the memory brings a smile to your lips...your heart fills with warmth and delight at the thought...then follow your heart, because the heart always leans toward the sun.

Today, give yourself time to face the sunshine.

If four out of five people suffer from headaches, does that mean that the fifth person enjoys them?

The things that one most wants to do
are the things that are probably most worth doing.
Winifred Holtby

Seek that particular mental attribute which makes you
feel most deeply and vitally alive, along with which
comes the inner voice which says, "This is the real
me," and when you have found that attitude, follow it.
William James

To know what you prefer, instead of humbly
saying "Amen" to what the world tells you you
ought to prefer, is to have kept your soul alive.
Robert Louis Stevenson

Let us remember that within us there is a palace
of immense magnificence.
Teresa of Avila

RIDING HIGH

Two dog owners were talking at the dog park. One said, "I'm really irritated with my dog. He'll chase anyone on a bike."
"What are you going to do?" asked the other. "Take him back to obedience training?"
"No; I think I'll just take his bike away."

OFF TRACK

A commuter was sick and tired of his two-and-a-half-hour drive to work every day. "You should take the train," suggested a coworker.
"I did once," the commuter replied, "but I couldn't drive the thing to save my life!"

JUST THE WAY I AM

A cowboy walked into a blacksmith shop and casually picked up a horseshoe, not realizing that it had just come from the forge. He quickly dropped the horseshoe and shoved his hand in his pocket as if nothing had happened.
The blacksmith had noticed, however, and he said with a grin, "Kind of hot, hey, pardner?"
"Nope," the cowboy managed through clenched teeth. "Just doesn't take me long to look at a horseshoe."

TENNIS MATCH

Did you hear about the fellow who met up with his tennis partner to play doubles? It took them ages to find two other guys who looked like them.

PASSING THE TIME

Bored during a long flight, a scholar with encyclo-pedic knowledge woke up the sleeping man seated next to him and asked if he would like to play a game. "Here's how it goes, I'll ask you a question, and if you don't know the answer, you pay me five dollars. Then you ask me a question, and if I don't know the answer, I'll pay you fifty dollars."

"You're on," said the man.

So the scholar asked: "What's the distance from the earth to the moon?"

Stumped, the man handed him five dollars.

"Ha!" the scholar said. "The answer is 238,857 miles. Now it's your turn."

The man thought for a few minutes and then said: "What goes up a hill with three legs and comes down with four?"

For the next hour, the scholar racked his brain. Finally, he reached into his pocket and brought out his wallet. "Okay, so what's the answer?" he said as he handed over the fifty dollars.

The man said, "I don't know," pulled out five dollars, gave it to the scholar, and went back to sleep.

What's the Good Word?

Some of us find it hard to keep up with all the snappy expressions and trendy catch-phrases that go around. As soon as we've caught on to current jargon, it's no longer current. The middle-schooler's eye-roll... his indulgent sigh...her embarrassed yip of disbelief that such an antiquated syllable should cross our lips... and we know that what we've just uttered is out, passé, gone-gone. We may as well put on bloomers and ride in a horse-drawn buggy.

Words of kindness, comfort, consolation, and hope—now there are words that are never out of date! Even those among us who shrink at the mere whiff of sentimentality have to hear those words, too (maybe especially so). Everyone needs to hear words that still will have meaning a year...a decade...a lifetime from now. Words worth remembering when we're alone or troubled, sad or at a loss to know what to do. Words that communicate the heft and depth of human feeling...words that speak of unselfish desires, articulate genuine emotions, and share true wisdom.

You yearn to hear those words, and you also possess the privilege of saying them. Thoughtful, compassionate, and carefully chosen words are always in style...and even if someone acts as if they're dreadfully out-of-date, speak them anyway. It just so happens that you know something about timeless fashion that they don't (yet).

> *How come the signs that say*
> *"Slow Children" always show*
> *a picture of a running child?*

SPELL IT OUT

A zookeeper was looking for new animals, so he started a letter. "I would like two mongeese," he wrote. He decided that didn't look right, so he changed it to "two mongooses." But that didn't look right to him, either. Finally, he wrote: "I would like one male mongoose and his mate."

IS IT COMMUNICABLE?

A man went to the drug store and asked the pharmacist if she could give him something for hiccups. Immediately she reached across the counter and slapped him across the face.
Stunned, the man said, "What did you do that for?"
"Well, you don't have hiccups any more, have you?"
"I didn't have hiccups—my wife does!"

YOU ASKED FOR IT

Her arms loaded with bags of groceries, she was struggling to make it through the door of her apartment. When she saw a neighbor coming down the hallway, she said, "Hi, Jerry. Can you give me a hand here, please?"
Jerry stopped and gave the woman an enthusiastic round of applause.
"What are you doing?" she cried in exasperation.
"You asked for a hand," Jerry said, still clapping. "Here it is."

We have too many high-sounding words
and too few actions that correspond with them.
Abigail Adams

One word frees us of all the weight and pain of life:
that word is love.
Sophocles

The difference between the right word and the almost
right word is the difference between lightning
and the lightning bug.
Mark Twain

Hear the other side.
Augustine

Words to the wise...

- Always keep your words soft and sweet, because one day you may have to eat them.

- Those who say nothing, show a fine command of language.

- Where wisdom is perfect, words are few.

- A word out of season can mar a whole lifetime.

- Water and words are easy to pour, but impossible to recover.

- A wise man hears one word and understands two.

- One kind word has more power than a dozen threats.

- A second wind is what some speakers get when they say, "And now in conclusion..."

- A closed mouth catches no flies.

- Too much talk is bound to include errors.

- A statement once let loose cannot be caught by four horses.

- To talk without thinking is to shoot without aiming.

Get the Picture?

What picture pops to mind when you receive an invitation to, say, a company reception? A friend's game night? Dinner and a movie? If you picture yourself feeling awkward and uncomfortable...watching the clock...at a loss for things to say, that's probably exactly what will happen. That's the power of a picture!

While it's true that changing the picture in your head won't magically transform you into a social butterfly, it does show you what *could* happen and prompts you to think about ways you can help make it happen.

• Picture the people you likely will meet and think about topics of interest to them. See yourself holding your own in conversation, whether it's light-hearted or serious, celebratory or commemorative.

• Ask the host what games will be played, and then bone up on rules and strategies. Maybe you'll come across a few little-known facts about the game or its inventor that you can bring up during the evening.

• Focus on the other person when you're meeting someone one-on-one. Visualize yourself smiling, chatting, asking questions, and listening. Have mutually interesting topics in the back of your mind in case the conversation lags.

A positive idea of what could take place is the first step to turning an imaginary picture into a real-life pleasure.

Vision: It's what people say you have when you guess right.

IF YOU THINK SO

*A woman rushed into her physician's office. "Doctor,"
she wailed, "what am I going to do? My husband
thinks he's a refrigerator!"
"Well, why exactly does that bother you?" the perplexed doctor asked.
"Because when he sleeps with his mouth open, the
light keeps me up all night!"*

EITHER WAY

*"Where's your brother?" Mom asked.
"Well," the boy replied, "if the ice on the pond is as
thick as he thinks it is, he's skating. If it's as thin as I
think it is, he's swimming."*

CAN'T SEE IT

*Dad doubted his son's newfound resolve to work out.
Nonetheless, he took the teenager to the sporting
goods store where they looked at weight-lifting equip-
ment. His son's eyes lit up when he spied a particular-
ly nice set of weights. "Please, Dad," the boy begged,
"I promise I'll use them every day for at least an hour!"
"That's a major commitment," his father said.
"I know it is, but I'll stick to it, you'll see."
"And they're pretty expensive," Dad remarked as he
looked at the price tag.
"I'll use them," the boy said, "I promise."
Despite his misgiving, Dad bought the equipment,
the boy picked it up, and the two headed for the door.
Once out on the sidewalk, the boy stopped, looking
stunned. "You mean I have to carry this all the way to
the car?"*

In the Balance

Have you ever noticed how often magazine articles featuring scrumptious desserts are followed by pages and pages of dieting tips? The editors of those magazines are pretty smart—they know that you can have the best of both in moderation. A small indulgence keeps you happy and a little exercise keeps you healthy.

Take other things. It's said, "All work and no play makes Jack a dull boy"—or Jill a dull girl. All of us need work and responsibilities, because that's how we earn self-respect and most often, an income. We also need recreation so we can rest, play, and have fun. We need time alone to get in touch with ourselves and with God, and time among others to build friendships and share our skills and talents. We need to balance serious thinking with whimsical dreaming...time-tested guidelines with stepping out on our own.

If you find yourself consumed by work, how can you put balance back in your life? Even ten or fifteen minutes of attentiveness to your physical and spiritual needs would help counteract the stresses of work. If your days lack structure and purpose, what can you do to add meaningful commitments? Part-time or volunteer work might be your answer.

Life balance lets you more fully enjoy and appreciate all that life has to offer.

What do we mean when we say something is "out of whack"? What's a whack?

*Everything that exceeds the bounds of moderation
has an unstable foundation.*
Seneca

*Sweet words are like honey; a little may refresh,
but too much gluts the stomach.*
Anne Bradstreet

*Exactness and neatness in moderation is a virtue,
but carried to extremes, narrows the mind.*
François Fenelon

Enough is as good as a feast.
Proverb

*Be moderate in order to taste the joys
of life in abundance.*
Epicurus

THAT TAKES THE CAKE

*"I made a chocolate cake for the family last night,"
said a woman to her friend. "We ate half of it after dinner, and I put the other half away." The woman went
on to say, "The next day, I couldn't stop thinking about
that cake. I allowed myself a small sliver, and then
another and another, until the cake was completely
gone." She was upset with her lack of willpower, and
embarrassed to confess to her family what she had
done.*

*"So what did they say when they found out?" asked
the friend.*

*"Oh, they never did," the woman said. "I made anoth-
er cake and ate half!"*

PERFECT 10

*A week before his wife's birthday, hubby asked her
what she would like most. "Oh," she replied dreamily,
"I'd love to be 10 again." Throughout the following
week, the eager-to-please husband gathered everything he'd need for a "Perfect 10" celebration.*

*When her special day arrived, his wife woke up to a
breakfast of chocolate chip pancakes topped with
whipped cream. That morning they visited a theme
park, rode the merry-go-round, ate hot dogs and
cotton candy, and stopped by the playground on their
way home. After a pizza dinner, they settled down to
watch a couple G-rated movies.*

*Only then did she turn to hubby and say, "Thank you,
honey; this was really a fantastic day. But what I really
meant was my dress size."*

Fresh Results

It's not very easy to change the way we do things—even when we find, time after time, that what we're doing doesn't work. Though experience might tell us we should try a new approach, we tend to go with what our parents did, what we've seen others do, or what we believe others expect of us. Or we're simply on autopilot—we don't stop and think before we speak and act. Yet if we keep on doing the same old things, we'll keep on getting the same old results.

Of course there's no point in doing things differently just for the sake of doing things differently. "If it's not broken, don't fix it" is good to remember, because we've lived long enough to learn what works and keep on doing it. But if we're dissatisfied or bored with the results of something we find ourselves doing over and over again, it *is* broken. No doubt about it.

Consider another approach you might take to the situation that always ends up with you upset or angry—a particular social setting, the unthinking behavior of others, an explosive topic of conversation that someone is bound to bring up. What if you met it differently? What if you *didn't* say what you always say? What if you *didn't* react the way you always react?

> *If a boomerang always comes*
> *back to you after you throw it,*
> *why throw it in the first place?*

NOT AGAIN!

Every Sunday, the same two young brothers acted up in church. No amount of disapproving looks from their parents and others parishioners or stern lectures and enforced time-outs at home seemed to have any effect. So one Sunday afternoon, their mother sent them to see the pastor in his office. The pastor called the eldest boy in first. He sat him down, looked him straight in the eye, and said, "Son, do you know where God is?"

The boy sat there in silence.

Again the pastor said, this time more forcefully: "Do you know where God is?"

The boy trembled but said nothing.

Leaning across his desk, the pastor asked one more time: "Do you know where God is?"

Terrified, the boy sprang from the chair and ran all the way home. The younger boy followed. Once at home with the door firmly shut behind them, the younger boy asked his brother what had happened in the pastor's office.

"God is missing," he said, "and they think we took Him!"

PRICE OF PAINTING

When the patient saw the bill for the office visit, he was livid. He phoned the doctor and shouted, "You have a lot of nerve charging me $400 just to paint my throat!"

"What do you expect for $400?" the doctor replied, "wallpaper?"

*Of all the paths a man could strike into, there is,
at any given moment, a best path.*
Thomas Carlyle

*First say to yourself what you would be;
and then do what you have to do.*
Epictetus

*Results! Why, man, I have gotten a lot of results.
I know several thousand things that won't work.*
Thomas Edison

It is not enough to aim; you must hit.
Proverb

*Any man may make a mistake,
but none but the fool will continue in it.*
Cicero

Do not look where you fell, but where you slipped.
Proverb

Patient: Doctor, I'm terribly nervous. This is the first operation I've ever had.
Surgeon: I know how you feel. This is the first operation I've ever done.

Mom: Son, you've got to be fair. Let your brother have a turn with the skateboard.
Son: Mom, he does get his turn! I ride it down the hill, and he rides it up the hill.

Customer: When I bought this car, you guaranteed that you would fix anything that broke.
Car dealer: That's absolutely correct, sir.
Customer: Well, I need a new garage.

Judge: Is this the first time that you have been up before me?
Defendant: I don't know, your honor. What time do you get up?

Teacher: Please don't whistle while you're studying!
Pupil: I'm not studying, ma'am, just whistling.

Patient: How much will it cost to have this tooth pulled?
Dentist: Fifty dollars.
Patient: You charge fifty dollars for thirty seconds of work?
Dentist: Well, if you prefer, I can work more slowly.

How You See It

"You're as young as you feel," the saying goes. And it's certainly true! Despite what the mirror tells them or the number of candles on their birthday cakes, many seniors say they feel no different than they did ten, twenty, or even thirty years ago. But they often notice this: Younger people often perceive them as slow, weak, or out of touch with today's world.

Yet let's think back to our own early years. Our eyes locked on to other young faces. We identified with our peers, who were also going to school, seeking relationships, starting careers and families. Outside of the older people who were part of our family circle or were directly involved with us, we probably took little notice of the sixty-year-old in the supermarket, the seventy-year-old who lived down the street, or the eighty-year-old stranger. It's just human nature. As we forgive ourselves, we can also smile and forgive the young eyes that seem to look right through us. We know!

And we know this, too: No matter what age we are, no one's perception of us matters more than our perception of ourselves. We are as loved by God as we ever were. We are a necessary counterbalance to youthful haste and impulsiveness...a stable presence in a rapidly changing world...a graceful example of growing older, wiser, and better.

The best way to look young is to hang out with very old people.

So they say...

- Although cosmetic surgery might take ten years off your appearance, it won't do anything for a flight of stairs.

- The first sign of old age is when you hear snap, crackle, and pop, and it isn't coming from your breakfast cereal.

- By the time you reach your 80th birthday, you've learned everything. Your challenge now is to remember it.

- She loves to wear antique jewelry. Of course, when she got it, it was new.

- When he talks about his memories of Washington, people ask, "Do you mean the city, the state, or the general?"

- She's been pressing forty so long it's pleated.

- Old age is when you find yourself using one bend-over to pick up two things.

- It's been proven that age is contagious. It comes from birthday candles.

- By the time we learn to watch our step, we're not stepping out very often.

- Here's the secret of eternal youth: Lie about your age.

- She really doesn't mind getting older, but her body's taking it badly.

- They don't make mirrors like they used to. All the ones we buy now are full of wrinkles.

*Wrinkles should merely indicate
where smiles have been.*
Mark Twain

*To know how to grow old is the master-work
of wisdom, and one of the most difficult chapters
in the great art of living.*
Henri-Frédéric Amiel

*To be seventy years young is sometimes far more
cheerful and hopeful than to be forty years old.*
Oliver Wendell Holmes, Sr.

No wise man ever wished to be younger.
Jonathan Swift

*If wrinkles must be written upon our brows,
let them not be written upon the heart.
The spirit should never grow old.*
James A. Garfield

AS EXCUSES GO...

The elderly driver was pulled over by a highway patrol officer who noted that she was traveling well over the speed limit. But she talked herself out of a ticket by explaining to the officer that she had to get to her destination before she forgot where she was going.

LIKELY POSSIBILITY

At the end of the interview, the reporter said to the ninety-nine-year-old man, "Sir, it was great talking to you. I hope I can come back next year and interview you on your one hundredth birthday."

"I don't see why not," said the senior citizen. "You seem in pretty good health."

JUST THE FACTS

A census taker asked the homeowner how old she was. The woman seemed reluctant to answer, and then said, "Did Carl and Dora Hill next door tell you how old they are?"

"Yes, she did."

"In that case," the woman said, "I'm the same age."

"All right," the census taker said as he filled in the form. "I'll put that you're as old as the Hills."

You know you're getting on when...

- Someone compliments you on your alligator shoes, but you're not wearing any shoes.

- You can remember when eggs, bacon, fresh air, and sunshine were good for you.

- You stoop down to put on your shoes and wonder what else you can do as long as you're down there.

- Your children begin to look middle-aged.

- You remember when everything was fields and pastureland.

- The first candle on your cake burns out before they get the last one lighted.

- The candles cost more than the cake.

- Your feet hurt, and you haven't even stepped out of bed yet.

- Your kids' history lesson is on something you studied in current events class.

- You remember versions of songs the first time around.

- Your knees buckle but your belt won't.

- They roast marshmallows over your birthday cake.

Brush with Fame

We'll never forget the day we heard the famous orator speak...stood in the presence of an eminent author, scholar, or theologian...watched a legendary actor or dancer perform...exchanged a few words with a renowned musician or artist. We remember the aura of empowerment that seemed to surround them, and felt inspired and uplifted in their presence.

Although fame comes to only a few of us, each one of us can live empowered lives—lives that inspire and uplift others. We might not be able to motivate millions with eloquent speeches, but we can encourage a struggling child...comfort a grieving widow...listen to an anxiety-stricken friend. Not everyone has the aptitude or knowledge to make a mark in education or the arts, but each of us possesses natural capabilities and learned skills. We have distinctive abilities that we can use to help others and to enhance our corner of the world.

People renowned for their greatness simply have empowered themselves to use everything they've been given to make the world a better place, a more delightful, beautiful place. All you need to do is empower yourself to do the same right where you are. Will you become famous? Will others clamor to take a selfie with you? Maybe or maybe not. But for sure, you will be an inspiration.

A good example is the most effective teacher.

Man in blessing others finds his highest fame.
Sara Josepha Hale

*My advice is to consult the lives of other men,
as one would a looking glass, and from thence
fetch examples for imitation.*
Terence

*No true and permanent Fame can be founded except
in labors which promote the happiness of mankind.*
Charles Sumner

*To set a lofty example is the richest bequest
a man can leave behind him.*
Samuel Smiles

*Applause is the spur of noble minds,
the end and aim of weak ones.*
Charles Caleb Colton

Getting to Know You

Some times of transition are marked and some are not. The marked ones are easy to identify—they're the joyful celebrations and the tearful leavings, the new addresses and the bright successes that periodically come into our lives. The unmarked transitions, however, are less discernible, at least at first. Often we may not even know exactly when it started to happen, but we come to the realization that we see ourselves and the world differently than we used to.

All too often we choose to ignore or deny what is taking place. Is it anxiety that makes us want to pull back from being true to our current selves? Is it fear that keeps us from embracing the natural maturing of the mind and spirit? Yet the longer we wait, the longer we put off discovering what means the most to us now...what we want to do and pursue now...what we're interested in now.

If you are blessed with a longtime friendship, perhaps from childhood, you would never expect your friend to be the same person she was when you met her in grade school. Why imagine that you're the same person you were in the past? Life is a series of transitions, and getting to know *you* is an exciting and ongoing experience.

Most people are standing on a mountain of gold looking at a pile of silver in the distance.

We must always change, renew, rejuvenate ourselves;
otherwise we harden.
Johann von Goethe

Readjusting is a painful process,
but most of us need it at one time or another.
Arthur Christopher Benson

Everyone must row with the oars he has.
Proverb

The highest and most profitable learning
is the knowledge of ourselves.
Thomas à Kempis

It is in changing that things find purpose.
Heraclitus

GOOD NEWS, BAD NEWS

*The drill sergeant announced to the new recruits:
"Today I have some good news and some bad news.
First, the good news. Private Smith will be setting
the pace on our morning run." A murmur of approval
rippled through the platoon, as Smith was the slowest
runner of the group. Then the sergeant continued:
"And now the bad news. Private Smith will be driving
a truck."*

LET'S GO!

*A guy was lonely, so he decided that he would like
to have a pet. He went to the pet store and told the
owners that he'd like an unusual pet to keep him
company. After a great deal of discussion, the man
bought a centipede, along with a little white box to
keep it in. He took his purchases home, found a good
location for the centipede's abode, and put the critter
inside. Later that evening, he thought he'd take his
new friend with him to the coffee shop. "Say, want to
get a cup of coffee with me?" he asked the centipede
in the box. Hearing no answer, he asked again, "Let's
go out and grab a cup of coffee, okay?"
Again there was no answer, and the man was per-
turbed. Putting his face up against the centipede's
box, he shouted: "Do you want to go get some coffee
or not?"
A little voice came out from the box: "I heard you the
first time! I'm putting my shoes on!"*

Just for Pun

- The chicken crossed the road—it was poultry in motion.

- The seismologist discovered that her theory of earthquakes was on shaky ground.

- Ice is one of the few things that's really what it's cracked up to be.

- A village is a small town where everyone knows the trouble you've seen.

- A kangaroo is an animal that carries her brood in a snood.

- "Ouch!" is the class yell of experience.

- Salt is very useful in a pinch.

- The husband was proud of his new yacht, but his wife looked at it as floating debt.

- She regarded waffles simply as pancakes with a nonskid surface.

- The opera tryouts were two hours of trial and aria.

- Although his doctor was a quack, the patient still couldn't duck the bill.

- Whenever a ghost gets lost in a fog, he's mist.

Careful!

"Careful! Careful!" Most of us have heard those words from babyhood on—when we began to pull ourselves up on two feet by holding on to our parents' coffee table...when we were allowed to cross the street by ourselves...when we began to drive. Being careful helped save us from avoidable harm and danger.

As adults, the words still echo in our mind as we make decisions about how to spend our money, where to live and work, whom to allow into our lives, and how to protect our personal information. This, too, goes a long way to keep us safe and secure.

But there are times when "Careful! Careful!" can hold you back from the true adventures and discoveries that life presents to you. An opportunity, say, to go on a once-in-a-lifetime trip with family and friends...a chance to break away from what you've always known and follow a completely different path...the prospect of learning new things, making new friends, exploring new worlds. Yet there's a certain level of unease attached; careful, careful!

There's not always a "perfect" time to do something, and opportunities come with risk. You might pass one up for very valid reasons, and that speaks well for your wisdom and maturity; but if the only reason you can think of is, "I've got to be careful," then it might be time to carefully reconsider your answer.

Nothing ventured, nothing gained.

GOOD REASON

A ranch owner noticed that one of his ranch hands was out working in the field without earmuffs, despite a raw and biting winter wind. So the owner thought he would do the right thing by giving the man a pair of good-quality earmuffs. On another bitter cold day the following week, the ranch owner noticed that the man wasn't wearing the earmuffs that he had given him.

"Don't you like the muffs?" the owner asked.

"They're the warmest, most comfortable pair I've ever worn," the man replied.

"Then why aren't you wearing them?"

"Because," the man said, "I was wearing them the first day you gave them to me. Then Smith came along and offered to buy me lunch, and I didn't hear him! Never again! Never again!"

THE TALKING DOG

Al sees a sign in front of a farmhouse: "Talking dog for sale–$10." Intrigued, Al rings the doorbell and asks the farmer to show him the dog. When the dog appears, Al says, "So tell me about yourself."

The dog answers, "My ability was identified by the CIA when I was a pup. I worked with the agency for years, jetting around the world, sitting in on secret meetings, gathering vital information, and telling my handler back home. Later I got involved with the FBI, providing essential intelligence that let them crack several high-profile cases. After I was wounded in the line of duty, I retired. Right now, they're making a movie about my life."

Amazed, Al looks at the farmer. "Why on earth are you selling the remarkable dog for only $10?"

"Because he doesn't tell the truth," the farmer says. "He hasn't done any of that stuff."

*The fishermen know that the sea is dangerous and
the storm terrible, but they have never found these
dangers sufficient reason for remaining ashore.*
Vincent van Gogh

*Few are they who have never had
a chance to achieve happiness—
and fewer those who have taken that chance.*
André Maurois

*For of all sad words of tongue or pen,
the saddest are these: It might have been.*
John Greenleaf Whittier

Adventure is worthwhile in itself.
Amelia Earhart

All life is an experiment.
The more experiments you make, the better.
Ralph Waldo Emerson

In any moment of decision, the best things you can do
is the right thing, the next best thing is the wrong thing,
and the worst thing you can do is nothing.
Theodore Roosevelt

We see the brightness of a new page
where everything yet can happen.
Rainer Maria Rilke

I've always wanted to be...

- An angel, and I'm always harping on it.

- An astronaut, but everyone told me I need to come down to earth.

- A mountain climber, because it's the only way to stay in peak condition.

- A sewing teacher, but no one could get my point.

- An electrician, until Dad said, "Wire you doing this?"

- A meteorologist, and I was right as rain.

- A watchmaker, and I'm really wound up about it.

- A photographer, and it happened in a flash.

- An expert crossword puzzler, but I didn't have a clue how to start.

- An optometrist, until I made a spectacle of myself.

- A veterinarian, and I am pursuing it doggedly.

- A sculptor, even though I don't fit the mold.

What's Cookin'?

"If you can't stand the heat," Harry S. Truman once said, "stay out of the kitchen." And many of us do just that. Sticking around isn't pleasant when tempers boil over, insults spatter the conversation, nerves turn raw, resentment simmers, feelings scorch, and half-baked ideas are served up as a complete meal.

It just might be our willingness to stand the heat and stay in the kitchen, however, that works to lower the temperature. We can be the ones who speak calming words of moderation...provide the cool air of patience and compassion...offer the sweet grace of a smile that leads to sprinkles of laughter. We can help cook up something everyone can enjoy, like the assurance that each person is loved and valued. We can offer the confidence that forgiveness, understanding, empathy, fairness, and goodwill always taste good.

Don't fear the heat. If you ignore or run away from the "heat" of your own inner conflicts or the struggles you are having with someone close to you, your discomfort will only intensify...and so will the heat. Before things boil over, be the one to pull the pan off the stove. Be the one who refuses to fan the flames, who has a better recipe. Be the one with the courage it takes to stay in the kitchen.

Anger is one letter short of Danger.

*In case of any difficulty remember that God has pitted
you against a rough antagonist that you may be a
conqueror, and this cannot be without toil.*
Epictetus

*If you yield to adversity,
the chances are it will master you,
but if you recognize in yourself the power of mastery
over conditions, then adversity will yield to you.*
Ralph W. Trine

*It is not until we have passed through the furnace
that we are made to know how much dross there
is in our composition.*
Charles Caleb Colton

*All problems become smaller
if you don't dodge them, but confront them.*
William F. Halsey

*Conquering any difficulty always gives one a secret
joy, for it means pushing back a boundary line
and adding to one's liberty.*
Henri-Frédéric Amiel

NO KITCHEN SHOULD BE WITHOUT…

- *A big basket of calm and a large jar of peace*
  set out for all to see

- *A full measure of words that sound soft and sweet,*
  with the aroma of kindness and love

- *Plenty of time to listen*
  to young and old and everyone in between

- *Plenty of room for inviting*
  friends both near and far

- *Laughter by the bagful—always keep in stock!—*
  And smiles by the spoonful, ever right at hand

- *Ingredients you can depend on for their freshness,*
  quality, truth, and taste

   Have these always in your "kitchen"
   And serve to friends and family
   each day throughout the year.

Listen Up!

How annoying to find that a person isn't listening to us when we're trying to tell them something! It's *very* annoying. We might be excused for finding someone else to talk to, someone who will take a genuine interest in what we have to say. But guess who *we* often ignore? Ourselves.

That little voice inside us that warned us to watch our step? We shushed it up, ran full speed ahead, and then wished we had paid attention to what it wanted to tell us. The hunch we had that perhaps not everything was quite as simple and easy as is appeared? Turns out our hunch was right, and we would have saved ourselves a lot of grief if we had taken a few moments to listen to ourselves.

Our gut reactions are worth hearing out. They're the words of our heart, and when we refuse to listen to our heart, we're ignoring ourselves. We're allowing our impulses to cancel our principles, our desires to overcome our dignity, our present-day wants to undercut our future well-being. A hunch can be the voice trying to tell us what our spiritual vision perceives, and it's far deeper than what our outer eyes can see. That wait-a-minute feeling that seems to come from nowhere? It just might be a whisper from heaven.

Listen, because you're well worth listening to.

Life is a school where you learn how to remember what your soul already knows.

When conscience is our friend, all is at peace;
however, once it is offended,
farewell to a tranquil mind.
Mary Wortley Montagu

The voice of conscience is so delicate
that it is easy to stifle it: but it is also so clear
that it is impossible to mistake it.
Madame de Staël

Trust the instinct to the end,
though you can render no reason.
Ralph Waldo Emerson

And after the earthquake a fire; but the Lord was not
in the fire: and after the fire a still small voice.
1 Kings 19:12

NOW HEAR THIS!

"The car won't start," said a wife to her husband.
"I think there's water in the carburetor."
Hubby chuckled and said, "Honey, how do you know
there's water in the carburetor? Why, I'm surprised
that you even know what a carburetor is!"
"I'm telling you," the wife stated firmly, "there's water
in the carburetor."
"Okay, let's go take a look," hubby said as he got up
from his chair. "So where's the car?"
"In the swimming pool."

THEN AND NOW

"Young man," said the judge to the defendant,
"where do you work?"
"Here and there," said the man.
"What is it you do for a living?"
"This and that," said the man.
"Take him away!" ordered the judge.
"Wait a minute!" the man protested. "When will I be
let go?"
The judge replied, "Sooner or later."

The Value of Things

Perhaps we're never as smart, sophisticated, stylish, and chic as we were when we were twenty-one. We could tell anyone (especially our parents) what was In and what was out, what was classy and what was kitschy, and what those-in-the-know knew (us) and what those-in-the-dark so sadly lacked (everyone else).

Then comes the day you visit Mom and Dad's home and notice the once-scorned painting still hanging over the fireplace...those decidedly tacky knick-knacks that have always sat in the china cabinet. Suddenly they take on a new meaning, an incomparable value, because these familiar objects were part of your past. They had a place year after year in family celebrations, and now perhaps your own children are seeing them every Christmas, every Easter, every summer. Tender feelings sweep over you...here are *valuable antiques*. Heirlooms. Objects of sentimental attachment.

Somehow being on the cutting-edge doesn't mean much anymore. You don't know exactly when your feelings changed, but the smile of acceptance comes so easily now...the warmth of remembrances satisfy so completely now...the presence of those old familiar objects brings on so many heartwarming memories now. You might not even try to tell the youngsters at your side who wonder why you're staring so intently at a mediocre piece of artwork...an unremarkable figurine. It's something they'll discover for themselves, years and years down the road.

Wise people can change their minds;
fools, never.

We do not succeed in changing things according to our desire, but gradually our desire changes.
Marcel Proust

Cleverness is not wisdom.
Euripides

Good judgment comes from experience, and a lot of that comes from bad judgment.
Will Rogers

The absurd man is he who never changes.
Auguste-Marseille Barthélemy

Wisdom is oftentimes nearer when we stoop than when we soar.
William Wordsworth

A man should never be ashamed to own that he has been in the wrong, which is but saying, in other words, that he is wiser today than he was yesterday.
Jonathan Swift

The world is quite right.
It does not have to be consistent.
Charlotte Perkins Gilman

To hold the same views at forty as we held at twenty
is to have been stupefied for a score of years
and to take rank, not as a prophet, but as an
unteachable brat, well birched and none the wiser.
Robert Louis Stevenson

Do I contradict myself? Very well then, I contradict
myself (I am large, I contain multitudes).
Walt Whitman

Today is not yesterday; we ourselves change; how can
our works and thoughts, if they are always to be the
fittest, continue always the same?
Change, indeed is painful, yet ever needful.
Thomas Carlyle

I wish to say what I think and feel today, with the
proviso that tomorrow perhaps I shall contradict it all.
Ralph Waldo Emerson

What Work?

We like to save ourselves extra work. That's the point of all those labor-saving appliances that we couldn't do without in the kitchen...box mixes that line the pantry shelves...washer and dryer that sit in the laundry room...vacuum cleaner that's stashed in the hall closet...and let's face it: remote control tucked right next to our favorite chair in the den. Few of us choose to spend time and effort on work we don't need to do!

Yet many of us continue to work, and work steadily and strenuously, on something that we don't need to do, nor can do—and that is, connect with God. We struggle to find a way to Him, and we spend countless hours laboring for His love...wondering if we've done enough to please Him...listening to anyone who claims to have the secret path to His presence and goodwill.

Here's not only a labor-saving truth, but a labor-ending one: God has done all the work. He has found you before you even knew you were lost, called you by name, and invited you to a close, personal relationship with Him. There's nothing left for you to do but say "yes" to the great mystery and magnificent love of God—not because of your endless effort, but because of His infinite power and all-encompassing love.

If you lose God,
it is not God who is lost.

A LITTLE EXTRA

The CEO of a major corporation was scheduled to deliver the keynote address at a convention. Hoping the occasion would boost his status and importance among his peers, he asked his public relations officer to write him a punchy twenty-minute presentation. When he returned from the event, however, he was livid. He burst into the speechwriter's office and shouted, "What's the big idea of giving me an hour-long speech? Most people walked out on me before I was even halfway through!"
The speechwriter was mystified. "I wrote you a twenty-minute speech," he said. "I also gave you the two extra copies you asked for."

HARD WORK

The interviewer at a retail clothing store was reviewing an applicant's résumé. He noticed that the man had never worked in retail before. "For someone with no experience," he told the applicant, "you are certainly asking for a high starting salary."
"You know," the applicant replied, "that work is so much harder when you don't know what you're doing."

*God is concealed from the mind
but revealed in the heart.*
Proverb

God enters by a private door into every individual.
Ralph Waldo Emerson

*The very best and utmost attainment in this life
is to remain still and let God act and speak in thee.*
Meister Eckhart

God loves each of us as if there were only one of us.
Augustine

God is love.
1 John 4:8

Everybody's Business

Have you noticed that the phrase, "It's none of my business," is usually followed by the word "but"? And then we'll hear (or supply) the rumors, details, and speculations that are indeed none of our business. Few of us have gone through life without discovering for ourselves the damage gossip can do to relationships and the hurt it can inflict on the human soul.

But MYOB doesn't mean turning a blind eye to the suffering of others, nor does it let us gloss over ugly facts when we become aware of them. There are times when someone else's business is our business, as when a friend is trapped by addiction or smothered by depression...a neighbor is overwhelmed by loss, sorrow, or hardship...a community is devastated by natural disaster, or plagued by unrelenting misfortune...individuals or groups are victimized by criminal activity. Is this our business? Yes, it is.

When their business is your business, too, you can pray. If appropriate, you might be able to extend financial assistance, or give of your time to alleviate suffering. You might find a way to offer something that shows that their anguish is your anguish...their sorrows are your sorrows...their business is your business, in the very best sense. Because when it comes to what's happening to one of us, it's the business of all of us. No "buts" about it!

Service to others is the rent
we pay for our place on earth.

*Joy can be real only if people look upon their life
as a service, and have a definite object in life
outside themselves and their personal happiness.*
Leo Tolstoy

*What do we live for if not to make the world
less difficult for each other?*
George Eliot

*Desire to sow no seed for your own harvesting;
desire only to sow that seed, the fruit of which
shall feed the world. You are a part of the world;
in giving it food, you feed yourself.*
Mabel Collins

They serve God well, who serve His creatures.
Caroline Norton

*Do all the good you can,
by all the means you can, in all the ways you can,
in all the places you can, at all the times you can,
to all the people you can, as long as you can.*
John Wesley

Have you heard?...

- Gossips usually get caught in their own mouth-trap.

- Those who gossip with you will gossip about you.

- Gossips have a keen sense of rumor.

- What you don't see with your eyes, don't witness with your mouth.

- Gossipy monkeys are blab-boons.

- Gossip is nothing more than halitosis of the mind.

- Those who speak much are much mistaken.

- A gossip is a newscaster without a sponsor.

- Gossip is a negative that has been developed and enlarged.

- A gossip is someone who suffers from a case of acute indiscretion.

- Gossip travels quickly through the sour grapevine.

NEIGHBORHOOD EVENT

A woman was holding a garden party on her patio, which overlooked a beautifully landscaped yard. During the event, two gardeners were weeding in a flower bed when suddenly one of them leaped high into the air and spun around.

Quite impressed with the man's feat, a guest said to the hostess, "I'll pay him five hundred dollars to perform at my next party!"

The hostess called the other gardener over and relayed her guest's proposal. "Hey, Al," the man shouted, "do you think for five hundred bucks you could step on that rake again?"

NEW KID IN CLASS

Out on the playground, the new boy in the sixth-grade classroom sat down next to a little kindergartener.

"Don't you think the principal is a dummy?" he asked the little girl.

"Say," she said, "do you know who I am?"

"No," the boy replied. "I just got here."

"Well, I'm the principal's daughter."

"Oh," said the boy. After a pause, he asked, "So do you know who I am?"

"No, I don't," she said.

"Thank goodness!" he exclaimed.

Try It!

What would you do if you were guaranteed not to fail? Maybe a tackle a skill you've always wanted to learn...a sport you think you'd enjoy, but never made time to get involved in...a subject you wish you knew more about, but have never made a serious attempt to do so.

Perhaps there has been no real opportunity, or there are legitimate and insurmountable limitations that stand between us and our ideas. But sometimes there's simply the fear of failure. We don't want to discover that we're unable to achieve what we had hoped, or find ourselves less-talented or less-expert than others. And who wants to be a quitter? So we decide not to be a starter, either.

Now for another question: So what if you quit? What's the big deal if you find that you really don't care for painting, have no particular talent for playing the piano, or that philosophical discussion really isn't your thing? At least you know because you tried, and that's more than you could say if you had never gone beyond thinking about it. But chances are excellent that following your natural interest will yield hours of pleasure, the pride of achievement, the joy of new friends, and continued personal growth. There's no guarantee, of course—but it's well worth a try!

Any age is the right age to start doing.

Have you ever wondered...

- What saxophones would look like if our elbows bent the other way?

- What the cured ham had?

- How the "Do Not Walk on the Grass" signs got there?

- How you can tell if you're running out of invisible ink?

- Why economy-size means small in cars and large in detergent?

- How a grapefruit knows where your eye is?

- How you would know if a word in the dictionary is misspelled?

- Why thirst-quenchers are sold in 64-oz. bottles?

- What a farmer does if his rooster comes down with laryngitis?

- How they'd measure hail if golf had never been invented?

- Does a shepherd get a staff discount?

- Why you can't hear mime artists if actions speak louder than words?

If you want to do something, do it!
Plautus

Can anything be sadder than work left unfinished?
Yes; work never begun.
Christina Rossetti

"But" is a fence over which few leap.
Proverb

Everyone who got where he is
had to begin where he was.
Robert Louis Stevenson

Flawed Feelings

On a scale of one to ten, few of us would rate ourselves a perfect ten. Unless we possess a really, really heightened sense of self-admiration, we look in the mirror and find flaws that enlarge in our eyes, but barely even register in someone else's. Comparing ourselves to others, we cite our shortcomings with a persistence, vehemence, and certainty that we'd never direct toward anyone else, regardless of their real or perceived limitations.

So why submit yourself to such over-the-top scrutiny? Sure, there could be some things about yourself that you wish were different, but they aren't. Probably everyone you ever have met and ever will meet feels the same way about themselves. But if you allow yourself to feel inferior to them due to the insufficiencies you apply to yourself, you naturally hold back. You imagine that they wouldn't want to be friends with you since.... You feel they are judging you because... You don't want to reach out to them, as you can't believe they have any desire to reach out to you.

But what if they feel the same way? In many cases, that's the truth. They are focused on *their* perceived flaws, not yours. They haven't welcomed you because they believe there's no way you'd welcome them! It takes one of you—the brave one—to make the first move.

To love others,
we must first love ourselves.

STRAIGHT SHOT

Riding through the forest one day, a medieval noble-
man found several archery targets on trees with an
arrow stuck right in the center of each target. He was
mightily impressed with the marksmanship displayed,
and he instructed his servants to find the skilled
archer. When the servants returned from their search,
they had a small boy in tow. "Are you the one respon-
sible for these perfect hits?" asked the nobleman,
hardly believing his eyes.

"Yes, sire," the boy answered.

Suspicious, the nobleman asked: "Now you didn't just
walk up to the targets and jab the arrows in the center,
did you?"

"No, sire, I did not," the boy said. "I'm telling the truth
when I tell you that I shot the arrows from one hun-
dred paces away."

"I believe you," said the nobleman, "and therefore I
admit you into my service on an annual salary of fifty
gold sovereigns for the next ten years."

The boy was elated. "That is most generous of you,
sire!"

The nobleman patted the boy on the head and said
with an indulgent smile, "Now, son, tell me how you
came to become such an outstanding archer at so
young of an age."

"It didn't take all that much," the boy said. "First I
shoot the arrow at the tree, and then I paint the target
around it."

What you think about yourself is much more important
than what others think of you.
Seneca

To succeed is nothing—it's an accident. But to feel no
doubts about oneself is something very different:
it is character.
Marie Lenéru

The worst loneliness
is not to be comfortable with yourself.
Mark Twain

Let a man's talents or virtues be what they may,
we only feel satisfaction in his society
as he is satisfied in himself.
William Hazlitt

If God has wanted me otherwise,
He would have created me otherwise.
Johann von Goethe

Good for You

Some things just aren't going to work together. No matter how hard we try, we're not going to be able to convince someone to change who doesn't want to change. No matter how much we manipulate events to make our wishes a reality, there are many factors that are completely beyond our control. No matter how cleverly we plan our strategy, there are some battles that we're not going to win.

Though your intentions are good, your advice wise, and your actions helpful, you have concluded that he's not going listen to reason...she's far from giving up her chosen way of life...they're not going to give you the salary or promotion or position that you desire and deserve. Unfair, especially after you've done and said what you feel are all the right things. So now the time has come for you to stop struggling and accept the facts as they are. The time has come for you to do what's good for you.

It's good for you to let your loved one know that your door is always open...but you need to go forward with your own life. It's good for you to stand up for your proven abilities and find where you can best use your skill and talent. It's good—it's excellent—for you to remember that God can handle what you can't.

> *Results are what you expect;*
> *consequences are what you get.*

*Be willing to have it so. Acceptance of what
has happened is the first step to overcoming the
consequences of any misfortune.*
William James

No man can have society upon his own terms.
Ralph Waldo Emerson

*When you have got an elephant by the hind legs
and he is trying to run away, it is best to let him run.*
Abraham Lincoln

*We may fail of our happiness, strive we ever
so bravely; but we are less likely to fail if we measure
with judgment our chances and our capabilities.*
Agnes Repplier

*When we see ourselves in a situation which must
be endured and gone through, it is best to make
up our minds to it, meet it with firmness,
and accommodate everything to it in the best way
practicable. This lessens the evil, while fretting and
fuming only serves to increase your own torments.*
Thomas Jefferson

MUSIC TO MY EARS

A general asked his assembled men, "Who likes music?" Three recruits stepped forward, anticipating an invitation to an upcoming concert.
"Great," said the general. "I've just bought a piano. You, you, and you take it to my apartment on the fourth floor."

FINE

A driver appeared in court on a charge of parking his car in a restricted area. Asked by the judge if he had anything to say in his defense, the man said: "There shouldn't be such misleading signs in the city."
"What do you mean by that?" said the judge.
"I mean that the sign clearly said, Fine for Parking Here."

JUST ONE

A speeding driver was pulled over by a state trooper. The driver demanded to know why he alone was pulled over when he wasn't the only one speeding. The trooper replied, "Have you ever been fishing?" Perplexed, the driver said, "Yeah, sure."
"And so," the trooper said, "have you ever caught all the fish?"

What do you get if you cross...

A singer and a tall ladder? Someone who can hit the high notes.

A flock of sheep and a radiator? Central bleating.

An alligator and King Midas? A croc of gold

Poison ivy with a four-leaf clover? A rash of good luck.

A student and an alien? A being from another universe-ity.

Ponds and streams? Wet feet.

Computers and potatoes? Micro chips.

Parrots and pigs? Birds that hog the conversation.

A dog and a telephone? A golden receiver.

A mouse and a bottle of olive oil? A squeak that oils itself.

Elephants and fish? Swimming trunks.

A hairdresser and a bucket of cement? Permanent waves.

Right Size

Motivational speakers say it, and we may say it to our children and grandchildren: "Dream big!" We know that big dreams can drive the action, commitment, and perseverance necessary to make them come true.

At a certain life stage, however, we begin to evaluate our dreams in the light of experience and reality, maturity and wisdom. Perhaps our values have shifted—what we thought was necessary for happiness at 20 years of age may not be our understanding at 40, 50, or 60. Maybe we are discovering hidden talents and abilities, and they are taking us in a direction we could never have conceived of earlier in life. Often unforeseen events and opportunities invite us to dream new dreams, dreams that give our lives meaning and purpose.

There comes a time when we're ready to right-size our dreams and expectations. Far from a loss, it's a gain in contentment, acceptance, satisfaction, and fulfillment. We trade what we can't do for what we can do—for what we are doing, because we've grown to experience the grace, beauty, and privilege of being who we are and where we are at this moment.

Welcome dreams—big ones and little ones alike... but follow the ones that are exactly the right size for you.

When somebody tells you that nothing is impossible, ask him to dribble a football.

BUGGY EXPERIENCE

A troop of kids from the city were on their first camping trip. By evening, the mosquitos were out in full force, and the boys had to huddle under blankets to avoid being bitten. Then one of the kids saw a swarm of lightning bugs and said to his friend, "We might as well give up. They're coming after us with flashlights now."

THANKS TO ME

"So," Grandma asked her newly graduated granddaughter, "did you make the top half of the class." "No, Grandma," the graduate replied. "I'm one of the students who made the top half possible."

50/50 CHANCE

A student, completely unprepared for the teacher's pop quiz, decides to toss a coin up in the air. Heads, true; tails, false. Fifteen minutes later, he gets to the end of the quiz. But then he goes back to the beginning and starts flipping the coin again, sweating over each answer he had circled.
"Why are you going back over this?" asked the teacher.
"I'm rechecking my answers," says the student.

VOICE OF EXPERIENCE

A riverboat captain, wanting to put his passengers at ease, announced: "Ladies and gentlemen, I've navigated boats on this river for so long that I know where each and every sandbar is." Suddenly the boat struck a sandbar so hard that it shook the vessel and sent the passengers scrambling. "What'd I tell you?" the captain said. "There's one of them now!"

I cannot do everything, but still I can do something;
and because I cannot do everything,
I will not refuse to do something I can do.
Edward Everett Hale

I can't write a book commensurate with Shakespeare,
but I can write a book by me.
Walter Raleigh

If you aspire to the highest place, it is no disgrace
to stop at the second, or even the third, place.
Cicero

People are ridiculous only when they try
or seem to be that which they are not.
Giacomo Leopardi

No matter how much you push the envelope,
it will still be stationery.

Chasing your dreams does not count as exercise.

A bird in the hand
makes blowing your nose rather difficult.

Everything is within walking distance
if you have the time.

If you dream in color, is it a pigment of
your imagination?

If you dream that you're sleeping,
will you feel doubly rested in the morning?

Pick and Choose

Busy, busy, busy! We're expected to be busy and keep busy. Ask a friend how she's doing, and we're likely to hear a litany of activities she's involved in, commitments she has made, and responsibilities she has taken on—that is, before she rushes off to her next appointment!

While it's true that being productively busy helps keep us mentally sharp, emotionally grounded, purposefully occupied, and engaged with life, it's possible to find ourselves *too* busy. That's when we're running from place to place and event to event from sunup to sundown. There's no space in our waking hours to sit by ourselves and get in touch with our thoughts and feelings...no time to turn our attention to God in heartfelt prayer...no chance to have a leisurely chat with a loved one or sit down with a friend...no break to follow a hunch, ponder an idea, noodle through a complex issue, read a book, hear the trees rustle in the wind.

More important than how much you do is what you're doing. If it's neither necessary nor meaningful, it's time to let it go. If competing activities fight for your time, decide what you can do and what you cannot do. Learn to delegate. Learn to say "No." Know your priorities, and let yourself pick and choose how—and when—you will keep busy, busy, busy.

What's the use of running
if you're on the wrong road?

It is not enough to be busy. So are the ants.
The question is: What are we busy about?
Henry David Thoreau

One half of knowing what you want
is knowing what you must give up before you get it.
Sidney Coe Howard

We can outrun the wind and the storm,
but we cannot outrun the demon of Hurry.
John Burroughs

O Lord, may I be directed what to do
and what to leave undone.
Elizabeth Fry

You will never "find" time for anything.
If you want time, you must make it.
Charles Buxton

Well Cultivated

If you have a garden, you will always have something to do! Whether you're growing food for the table or cultivating flowers purely for their beauty, you know that keeping a garden hoed, weeded, and fertilized takes continuing work and attention. Without it, crops yield less, blossoms wane, buds wither, and thistles take over where healthy plants once grew.

Something else that takes constant tending is our relationships. Strong and vibrant relationships between family members, friends, coworkers, neighbors, and church members require perpetual care. We cultivate new relationships by being open to others, and we nurture longtime relationships by never taking them for granted...by feeding them with heartfelt thoughtfulness and genuine affection. We keep them free of weeds and thorns by quickly admitting when we're wrong and graciously granting forgiveness when others cause us offense.

Yes, it would be easy to put off phoning or emailing your friend. It would be simple to not invite into your home the family member who annoys you, and much simpler to ignore the coworker whose views are so different from yours. But a word of caution! The relationship you discount today could be the one that proves invaluable tomorrow.

Tend to your relationships as you would a prized garden. Do what you can to make your relationships grow and bloom, and they will bring you a lifetime of joy, pleasure, support, and happy memories.

The best vitamin
for developing friends is B1.

SOONER, PLEASE?

A librarian was sound asleep at two o'clock in the morning when her phone rang. The voice on the other end of the line said, "Ma'am, what time does the library open?"

"Nine o'clock," answered the bleary-eyed librarian. "Why in the world are you calling me at home at this time of night with a question like that?"

The caller sighed. "Not until nine o'clock, huh?"

"No!" the librarian said, now angry. "What's so important that you need to get into the library before nine o'clock?"

"Oh, I don't want to get in," said the caller. "I was asleep in the reading room when the library closed, and now I want to get out."

YOU'RE HIRED

Bill and Bob were applying for the same job, and they both took a written test. A few minutes after they had turned in their answers, the interviewer called the two of them into his office. "You both got the same number of answers wrong," the interviewer said, "but I'm hiring Bob."

"How come Bob gets the job," Bill protested, "since we had the same number of wrong answers?"

The interviewer said, "Because one of his wrong answers was better than yours."

True friends are those who...

- Walk in when the rest of the world walks out.

- Don't think it's a permanent condition if you make a fool of yourself.

- Couldn't care less if your socks don't match.

- Say nice things about you behind your back.

- Know you well and love you anyway.

- Accept you just as you are, but also invite you to grow.

- Ask how you are and wait for an answer.

- Understand how you feel, even though you haven't said a word.

- You know you can call at 4 a.m. and they wouldn't hang up.

- Help you see yourself more clearly.

- Laughs with you, but never at you.

- Are the kisses blown to you by angels.

Good People

"Things just can't get any worse," we sigh—and then they do. Headline after headline, news flash after news flash, delivers a stream of bleak stories and frightening images. It would be easy to simply throw our hands in the air in utter hopelessness! But most of us don't.

We go on about our daily lives, despite both the real and imagined chaos around us. We continue in the face of personal troubles, community unrest, national disasters, and world catastrophes. Most of us—yes, the majority of us—carry on without a thought to the courage and fortitude it takes to persevere day after day. We simply do it. Most of us love and laugh, irrespective of those voices and situations that instill fear in the heart. Most of us maintain our ideals, strive to build up, work for improvement, and look ahead in faith, even when reality makes the going difficult.

We celebrate the heroes who step forward in big ways to counteract the effects of calamity—to pick up the pieces, renew and strengthen communities, and restore the good that has been lost, perhaps with something even better. But don't forget to celebrate those who take on the day's work and responsibilities with firm resolution and human dignity. Celebrate those who inspire, encourage, and persevere. Celebrate you.

Hope is putting faith to work when doubting would be easier.

One man with courage is a majority.
Thomas Jefferson

*Even if I knew that tomorrow the world would go to
pieces, I would still plant my apple tree.*
Martin Luther

*Courage is resistance to fear;
mastery of fear—not absence of fear.*
Mark Twain

*To persevere, trusting in what hopes one has,
is courage. The coward despairs.*
Euripides

*Let nothing disturb you; let nothing frighten you.
All things are passing; only God never changes.*
Teresa of Avila

Patience and fortitude conquer all things.
Ralph Waldo Emerson

Go with the Flow

Remember your first crush? Maybe it happened in grade school when you looked across the room and found yourself mesmerized by sparkling eyes... shiny hair...a toothy grin. You could talk easily to anyone else, but you were shy around this one special classmate. You stole glances, fearing the class blabbermouth would pick up on your feelings and tell everyone...everyone, including.... No, you couldn't let that happen!

A favored few enjoy a long and happy life with their first loves. For the majority of us, however, our initial heart-flutter was only the beginning of many crushes, infatuations, passions, and oftentimes, genuine love. We've learned something along the way, and we're far from the naive child we once were. Yet gentle, joyful, innocent love can still flow through our heart like a sparkling stream...if we let it. Even as mature and experienced as we are, we still have the capacity to allow ourselves to give love...to receive love...to live in love, if we want it.

Because you know there are all kinds of love, you can love more fully...more deeply...more broadly...more completely. You've discovered the capacity of love, so you can experience what it's like not only to love a special person, but to love family and friends, your community, your world, and your God. And with God, there is no end of love for you.

Nothing beats love at first sight
except love with insight.

NOT YOU, DEAR

A husband was relaxing on the sofa watching a football game when he heard his wife's voice in the kitchen. "What would you like for dinner this evening, sweetie? Chicken, beef, or fish?" "Thanks, dear," he answered, delighted at her solicitude, "chicken would be great."

His wife stepped into the den. "Honey," she said, "I was talking to the cat."

DON'T FORGET!

One morning over breakfast a woman said to her husband, "Honey, I bet you don't know what day this is." "Of course I do," he indignantly answered as he tried to recall the dates of her birthday and their wedding anniversary. Still unsure but refusing to show it, he left for work.

At 11:00, the doorbell rang. When the woman answered it, she was handed a bouquet of a dozen long-stemmed red roses. At 1:00, the doorbell rang again and she found an ornate box of choice chocolates waiting for her. At 3:00, a carrier brought a gift card to her favorite boutique.

The woman couldn't wait for her husband to return home from work. "First the flowers, then the chocolates, and then the gift card!" she exclaimed as he walked in the door. "This is the best Groundhog Day I've ever had in my life!"

Many waters cannot quench love,
neither can the floods drown it.
Song of Solomon 8:7

Love is the most powerful and still the most unknown
energy of the world.
Teilhard de Chardin

Love is space and time measured by the heart.
Marcel Proust

Love is our highest word and the synonym for God.
Ralph Waldo Emerson

Give us, Lord,
A bit of sun,
A bit of work,
And a bit of fun.

ENGLISH PRAYER